$.50
6/28
EH

The Little School System That Could

D0813894

SUNY series, Educational Leadership

Daniel L. Duke, editor

The Little School System That Could

Transforming a City School District

Daniel L. Duke

STATE UNIVERSITY OF NEW YORK PRESS

Published by
State University of New York Press, Albany

Printed in the United States of America

For information, contact State University of New York Press, Albany, NY
www.sunypress.edu

Production by Kelli Williams-LeRoux
Marketing by Fran Keneston

Library of Congress Cataloging-in-Publication Data

Duke, Daniel Linden.
    The little school system that could : transforming a city school district / Daniel L.
Duke.
        p. cm. — (Suny series, educational leadership)
    Includes bibliographical references and index.
    ISBN 978-0-7914-7379-5 (hardcover : alk. paper)
    ISBN 978-0-7914-7380-1 (pbk. : alk. paper)
    1. School improvement programs—Virginia—Manassas Park—Case studies.
2. Education, Urban—Virginia—Manassas Park—Case studies.   3. Educational
change—Virginia—Manassas Park—Case studies.   I. Title.

LB2822.83.V8D85 2008
371.2009755'2372—dc22   2007024542

10 9 8 7 6 5 4 3 2 1

Dedication

Dedicated to Tom DeBolt and Frank Jones, for their vision and persistence in the service of Manassas Park's young people, and to Bruce McDade, for making his advisor proud.

Contents

Tables

Preface

What does it take to turn around a low-performing school system? That is the central question addressed in this organizational history of a small city school system in northern Virginia. It is also a question on the minds of politicians, policy makers, and educational leaders. The landmark No Child Left Behind Act and various state and local accountability initiatives have fostered an environment in which the continued operation of low-performing schools no longer is acceptable. Low-performing schools frequently are found in low-performing school systems. Manassas Park City Schools was such a system. From its creation in 1976 until 1995, the fledgling school system struggled with a variety of problems ranging from inadequate resources to deplorable facilities. Mismanagement, incompetence, and personnel turnover were common. These and other factors contributed to low staff morale and subpar student achievement.

Things began to change in 1995 when the Manassas Park School Board hired a new superintendent. How Tom DeBolt and his allies transformed the school system is a story to hearten even the most skeptical observer of public education. While the account of what happened in Manassas Park is most directly applicable to other small city school systems, it contains lessons for all school systems facing the challenges of low performance, underfunding, political turmoil, and a culture of low expectations and defeatism.

Recording a decade's worth of organizational change requires a good deal of assistance. Forty-five people contributed their insights and information to this study. They included local leaders, members of the staff of Manassas Park City Schools, consultants, and architects. I would like to express my appreciation to all of these individuals, especially Tom DeBolt, Frank Jones, Bruce McDade, Pam Blake, Lois Steele, Ritchie Carroll, Gail Pope, Virginia Bowerman, Pat Miller, Bill Bradley, and Bob Moje. Melissa Levy, a research assistant with the Partnership for Leaders in Education at the University of Virginia, was very helpful in collecting archival information. Patsy Craig deserves enormous credit for preparing the manuscript. Thanks also to Lisa Chenel for supporting this project from the beginning and to the two reviewers of the book. Finally, I wish to acknowledge the generous financial support of the Microsoft Corporation. Microsoft has taken an active interest in programs designed to promote school and school system turnarounds, including the University of Virginia's unique Partnership for Leaders in Education, a joint venture of the Curry School of Education and the Darden Graduate School of Business Administration.

Daniel L. Duke
Charlottesville, Virginia

Timeline of Important Events in the History of Manassas Park City Schools

1975   Manassas Park becomes an independent city.

1976   Manassas Park City Schools is created. Robert Strickland is chosen as the first superintendent.

1979   Strickland resigns. Robert Lewis becomes superintendent. Enrollment drops to 1,747 students.

1981   Lewis resigns.

1982   Gary Smith becomes superintendent.

1985   Smith resigns. Jimmy Stuart becomes superintendent.

1989   Stuart resigns. James Moyers becomes superintendent.

1991   Moyers resigns. David Martin becomes superintendent.

1995   Martin resigns. Tom DeBolt becomes superintendent. Plans for a new high school are presented to the school board. Enrollment drops to 1,561 students.

1996   DeBolt becomes active in local Republican Party.

1998   Virginia launches educational accountability initiative, including statewide standardized testing.

1999   The new Manassas Park High School opens. DeBolt begins campaign for a new elementary school.

2000   DeBolt conducts first retreat for his leadership team.

2001   Cougar Elementary School opens. School board approves a six-year long-range plan for the school system.

2004   City council adopts a revenue sharing agreement with Manassas Park City Schools. Three out of four Manassas Park schools achieve Adequate Yearly Progress under the No Child Left Behind Act. Leadership team develops new vision and mission statement.

2006   Renovated Manassas Park Middle School opens. School board and city council reach agreement on where to locate new elementary school.

Chapter 1

Introduction

Don't tell Tom DeBolt, the superintendent of Manassas Park City Schools in northern Virginia, that his school system cannot be world class. Don't point out that his working-class community has a modest tax base and a growing population of recent immigrants, many of whom speak little or no English. Don't argue that Manassas Park cannot possibly compete for talented teachers with its more prestigious and affluent neighbors. Don't try to persuade him that the most many of his students can hope for is to graduate from high school and find a blue collar job with decent wages. Tom DeBolt's ambitions would shame an alchemist, but in the case of Manassas Park, they are coming true!

DeBolt is a self-professed visionary and optimist, and the story of Manassas Park's transformation from a perennially low-performing school system with disreputable facilities and dispirited educators to a model small city school system with fully accredited schools, championship teams, acclaimed extracurricular programs, and award-winning school buildings is, first and foremost, a story of inspired and inspiring leadership. But it is much more. It is a saga of local politics, of a community rallying to support its beleaguered schools, and of the wonders that can be wrought through teamwork. What took place in Manassas Park between 1995 and 2005 was not just dramatic improvement in student performance on standardized tests, but the rebirth of an entire school system.

What does it take to transform a low-performing school system into a successful and respected enterprise? This question serves as the focus for *The Little School System That Could*. Like the tiny steam engine in the classic children's book, the Manassas Park City Schools (MPCS) demonstrated the power of positive thinking as it changed from a struggling school division to a symbol of educational improvement and a source of community pride. Created in the immediate aftermath of Manassas Park's establishment, in 1975, as Virginia's newest city, MPCS languished for two decades in the shadow of outstanding neighboring school systems in Fairfax County, Prince William County, Loudoun County, and Manassas City. Then in 1995, the Manassas Park School Board hired a new superintendent, Dr. Tom DeBolt. He inherited a collection of ramshackle schools, a budget that had not kept pace with enrollment growth or inflation, and a track record of academic and administrative problems. A decade later, every Manassas Park school had achieved state accreditation under the provisions of Virginia's tough educational accountability program, the school system had won architectural awards for its innovative school designs, Manassas Park teams had garnered league and even state championships, and salaries for teachers and school administrators had grown to be competitive with Manassas Park's far more affluent neighbors.

Manassas Park's ten-year journey from educational backwater to beachfront, however, was not an uninterrupted string of giant steps forward. As travels go, the path covered by the school system was less like the flight of an arrow than the meanderings of a moth. Despite periodic setbacks, though, DeBolt and his colleagues stayed the course, eventually overcoming obstacles, silencing critics, and achieving success.

How this study was conducted and the conceptual framework that guided it will be discussed in the next section. Covering these matters up front will allow the chronicle of Manassas Park's turnaround to be presented without interruption as a continuous narrative. Following a description of the study's methodology, several reasons why this study's findings are important will be noted. The introduction concludes with an overview of the remainder of the book.

UNDERSTANDING SYSTEMIC CHANGE

Historians of education have characterized the process of school reform as a matter of persistent "tinkering" (Tyack & Cuban, 1995). Examples of dramatic transformation are rare. While such an assessment is reasonable, it should not obscure the fact that systemic change, such as what took place in Manassas Park, does occur. The more that can be learned about the nature of such sweeping change, the better educators will be able to address the needs of low-achieving school systems. Understanding the complexities of systemic change, however, is no simple matter. Many researchers feel most comfortable when they gaze through a microscope, not a wide-angle lens. Microscopes permit researchers to isolate particular features and study them in detail. Systemic change, however, defies such an approach. Multiple lenses, each oriented to a different aspect of change, are required to grasp the process in all of its complexity.

In order to investigate the transformation of MPCS, four lenses, or conceptual frames, were employed. These frames were developed and described by Bolman and Deal in their classic treatise on the study of organizations, *Reframing Organizations* (1997). Each frame embodies a set of assumptions regarding how organizations operate and adjust to their circumstances. These assumptions serve to focus attention on particular aspects of an organization and the role they play in supporting or inhibiting change.

One frame concerns the structural dimension of organizations. This perspective assumes that organizations such as school systems exist to accomplish a particular mission and that they need to develop a structure to achieve that mission with a reasonable degree of success or else they are unlikely to survive. Elements of an organization's "structure" include its goals, policies, quality control mechanisms, decision-making processes, roles, and organizational units. By examining the Manassas Park City Schools through the structural lens, it will be possible to determine the extent to which the school system's transformation involved changes in priorities, policies, programs, and processes.

A school system is unlikely to be transformed by restructuring alone. Bolman and Deal's second "lens," the human resource frame, focuses on the people who staff the organization. The key assumption supporting this perspective is that organizational success depends on the extent to which employees find their work meaningful and satisfying. People in organizations, in other words, have needs that go beyond earning a salary. When they are treated well and valued for their contributions, the likelihood of achieving the organization's mission is greatly increased. To understand what happened in Manassas Park City Schools, therefore, it is also necessary to consider working conditions, opportunities for collaboration and professional growth, salary enhancement, and other matters of importance to school system employees.

All organizations exist within a greater context. A school system, for example, is located in a community, a state, and a nation. Each of these contexts makes certain demands on the school system and harbors certain expectations for its performance. In order to survive, organizations must find ways to adapt to these contexts. According to Bolman and Deal, such adaptation typically involves a political component. Key assumptions supporting the political frame are that organizations depend on resources and resources are almost always limited. Conflict can occur when organizations compete to acquire the resources necessary to achieve their mission. Political activity is the consequence of efforts by organizations to deal with conflict over scarce resources. Since it is unlikely that a school system such as Manassas Park can be transformed without additional resources, it is important to learn about the school system's efforts to mobilize support for change and the resources needed to achieve it.

The fourth of Bolman and Deal's frames is the most abstract. The symbolic frame focuses on the symbols that embody and represent an organization's culture. It is assumed that much of what goes on in organizations is important because of the meaning or significance people attach to it. Sometimes organizations are unable to accomplish all that they set out to do, but what they *try* to do and how they go about it can symbolize cherished beliefs and values. Organizational change cannot be fully understood without investigating the symbolism and meaning associated with it. In this study of Manassas Park's transformation, attention is devoted to assessing changes in organizational culture over the decade form 1995 to 2005 and what these changes have meant to the school system and the community.

By combining the four frames and studying the structural, human resource, political, and symbolic dimensions of organizational change, it is possible to gain a reasonably comprehensive understanding of what was involved in the transformation of the Manassas Park City Schools. How the study actually was conducted is discussed in the next section.

DOING ORGANIZATIONAL HISTORY

Historians of organizations prefer to begin with information about which they can be reasonably certain. The sorry state of Manassas Park's school facilities, educational finances, and academic performance in 1995 is a matter of record. Equally indisputable are the conditions and accomplishments of the school system in 2005. These factual "bookends" give rise to a question: What happened in Manassas Park between 1995 and 2005 that might account for such dramatic change?

The first step in answering this question involves a careful inventory of all the ways the school system in 2005 differed from the school system ten years earlier. Organizational historians tend to assume that dramatic improvements in school facilities, educational finances, and academic performance are unlikely without other, less obvious changes. Identifying these "changes behind the changes" provides the foundation for subsequent efforts to explain *how* the school system's transformation was accomplished.

In order to get at this deeper level of change, interviews were conducted with a variety of individuals who were associated with Manassas Park City Schools over the years from 1995 to 2005. They included the superintendent, a school board chair, central office personnel, school administrators, city officials, and consulting architects. Each interview entailed questions regarding changes in the school system, including changes in organizational structure, operations, funding, personnel, and programs. In addition to these relatively straightforward changes, individuals also were asked to comment on more subjective aspects of transformation, including changes in organizational culture and school-community relations. Besides interviews, school board minutes, newspaper articles, school improvement plans, accreditation reports, financial records, documents produced by the central office, and an excellent dissertation on the early history of the school system were reviewed. In addition, school system planning sessions, administrative retreats, and school design workshops over the years from 1999 to 2005 were monitored by the author.

Identifying the variety of changes that took place in MPCS between 1995 and 2005 presented one kind of challenge. A second, and more difficult, task involved accounting for these changes. In order to determine *how* changes were accomplished, the organizational historian must reconstruct events as they actually occurred, which is not necessarily how people remember them occurring. Primary source materials such as minutes and memos can be helpful, but they do not always include a full account of what actually took place. Individuals in key positions were asked to provide narratives, or what Deborah Stone (1989) refers to as "causal stories," of how particular changes were achieved and for what reasons. To get as accurate a reconstruction of events as possible, it may be necessary to compare accounts from various sources, a process sometimes referred to as triangulation. In most cases, a reasonable level of agreement across informants and documents can be achieved, but in a few instances all that can be reported is that there is conflicting information about what actually took place.

One strategy that can be helpful to organizational historians trying to cover changes over a number of years is the critical incident approach. This method assumes that there are simply too many events in the life of any relatively complex organization to permit complete coverage. Such an account, even if possible, would make for very dull reading. Organizational historians consequently rely on the selection of *critical incidents* in order to craft a narrative.[1] Critical incidents represent potential turning points in the development of an organization, points at which the organization might have moved in different directions. Critical incidents frequently involve debates over mission and goals, the search for resources, changes in leadership, and failure to accomplish desired objectives. While the four frames discussed earlier are helpful in detecting *what* changed in Manassas Park, investigating critical incidents offers insights into *why* and *how* these changes were accomplished.

Interviews, board minutes, and newspaper articles were used to compile a chronology of events in Manassas Park City Schools between 1995 and 2005. Using this chronology as a starting point, selected informants were asked to pinpoint events that they felt were critical in the transformation of the school system. Those events about which there was general agreement then were chosen as critical incidents and further inquiry was directed at determining the circumstances surrounding them.

WHY IS THE MANASSAS PARK STORY IMPORTANT?

Talk of improving public education evokes various images. Three such images are windmills, wishing wells, and wings. Those who see windmills when they look at low-performing school systems are fatalists. Windmills suggest a quixotic undertaking, admirable in intent but unlikely to succeed. Attempts at fixing school systems, for others, are more like tossing money in a wishing well. They *hope* something good will result, but they really don't expect much. Still others look at troubled school systems and see sets of wings to help young people escape the gravitational pull of poverty, crime, and low expectations. These individuals believe that, with the right educational design and the proper thrust, liftoff can be achieved. Such beliefs now reflect the thinking of Manassas Park educators and community leaders. But this was not always the case.

In recent years, researchers have devoted considerable attention to studying what it takes to turn around low-performing schools. Less is known, however, about the transformation of entire school systems. As the school system goes, so goes the school. It is unlikely, in other words, that school improvement can be sustained as long as the systems in which they exist remain dysfunctional. The Manassas Park story provides an account of nothing less than *school system turnaround*. Manassas Park may not be New York City or Los Angeles, but it faces many of the same challenges confronting larger cities. Besides, the United States is full of small cities like Manassas Park, often located in the shadow of great cities, that struggle to cope with a limited tax base, increasing diversity, and demands for greater educational accountability. The 2002 Census revealed that Manassas Park was one of 1,436 small cities with populations between 10,000 and 24,999 (2002 Census of Governments, 2002). The fact that Manassas Park has been able successfully to address many issues common to most city school systems offers hope to all who are committed to giving every urban child a reasonable chance of succeeding in life.

The Manassas Park story is especially instructive because it is not a fluke or some overnight miracle that is unlikely to be replicable. As the rest of this book reveals, the transformation of MPCS came about because of exceptional leadership, patience coupled with persistence, careful planning, caring and commitment on the part of educators and community leaders, and a willingness on the part of educational leaders to work within the local political arena on behalf of students.

ORGANIZATION OF THE BOOK

Chapter 2 describes the circumstances surrounding the creation of the city of Manassas Park and its school system. The chapter goes on to detail the struggles of the school system during its first two decades to secure adequate resources and provide a decent education to the youth of Manassas Park. Chapter 3 begins in 1995 with the hiring of Tom DeBolt, Manassas Park's seventh superintendent in twenty years. The conditions DeBolt faced are detailed along with his initial efforts to forge political alliances and ensure the construction of a new high school. The challenges surrounding the building of a new elementary school close on the heels of opening the new high school are discussed in chapter 4. The next chapter examines three keys to sustaining success in the improving school system—building a leadership team, developing a long-range plan, and negotiating a revenue sharing agreement with the city council. Chapter 6 focuses on the maturation of a new organizational culture in Manassas Park City Schools, a culture characterized by high expectations and professional confidence. Chapter 7 examines some of the questions that occupied Manassas Park educators as the first decade of Tom DeBolt's leadership drew to a close.

The last two chapters place the organizational history of MPCS in perspective. Chapter 8 returns to Bolman and Deal's four "frames" to see how each was important to understanding the school system's transformation. The final chapter discusses some of the "lessons" of this transformation for educators in low-performing school systems and students of organizational change.

Chapter 2

The Birth of a School System

On June 1, 1975, the community of Manassas Park left Prince William County to become Virginia's newest city. Plans then had to be made by the fledgling city council to create a school system the following year. The infancy and childhood of the Manassas Park City Schools make Oliver Twist's early years seem privileged in comparison. There were many times between 1976 and 1995, in fact, when residents wondered if the school system would survive. Edgar Schein, a well-known organization theorist, maintains that all organizations must confront and effectively address matters of external adaptation and internal integration in order to continue to exist. External adaptation concerns the need of every organization to adjust and respond to the needs of its environment. Internal integration, on the other hand, involves efforts within the organization to keep everyone focused on the mission and prevent entropy. This pair of challenges can become a leader's nightmare when what is done to deal with one challenge actually triggers or exacerbates problems in the other arena. Such was clearly the case for Manassas Park City Schools during the school system's first two decades.

This chapter describes the withering array of problems that faced the school system in the aftermath of its birth. First, however, a brief description is provided of the circumstances surrounding the formation of the city of Manassas Park. Next comes an account of the myriad issues that arose within the school system, issues that ranged from infighting and mismanagement to low morale and personnel turnover. The net effect of these problems was to call into question the wisdom of secession from Prince William County and its well-regarded school system.

Many of the internal problems faced by Manassas Park educators were a direct or indirect result of tensions and turmoil in the community and beyond. A discussion of these external issues, including shortages of resources and squabbling between the city council and the board of education, is provided. The chapter concludes with a brief review of David Martin's tenure as superintendent. Hired in July 1991, Martin represented the kind of leader who could arrest the school system's downward spiral and initiate the improvements necessary to address both internal and external challenges.

A NEW CITY AND A NEW SCHOOL SYSTEM

The name "Manassas" forever will be associated with two major battles of the Civil War, or what some Virginians insist on calling the War between the States. A little more than a century after these epic battles took place, another pair of struggles occurred on nearly the same ground. These involved the efforts of two towns in northern Prince William County—Manassas and Manassas Park—to secede from the county and become independent cities. In Virginia, cities enjoy the same status as counties, each having the authority to raise local revenues, operate public schools, and provide other public services.

What caused these two communities to seek separation from Prince William County? Money played a part, as did increasing population.[1] At least one local official also believed "stiff-necked pride" was a factor. Manassas acted first. The town council was dissatisfied with the services it received from the county in return for its substantial contribution to county revenues. Manassas accounted for more than one-tenth of Prince William's local taxes, but town fathers complained that residents received little in the way of fire, police, and rescue services. After the Prince William Board of Supervisors rejected Manassas's request for a revenue-sharing agreement, the town council began to explore the option of becoming a city. When consultants informed council members that becoming a city actually would lower taxes for residents, the latter group initiated the separation process. Aware that the state had passed a moratorium on the formation of new cities after June 1, 1975, Manassas's mayor signed the petition to become a city as of May 1, 1975.

Officials in Manassas Park had many of the same concerns as their neighbors. Their community also was growing, and their share of county revenues was perceived to be inadequate to provide the services necessary to keep pace with growth. When Manassas announced its intention to become a city, Manassas Park Town Council members convened a meeting and decided to petition Manassas to consolidate the two communities (Town Council Minutes, Manassas Park Town Council, April 23, 1975, p. 1). The petition was rejected, and to make matters worse, the local newspaper inflamed feelings in Manassas Park by publicizing the concerns of Manassas residents. According to the *Journal Messenger* ("Community Sound Off," April 30, 1975, p 4A), Manassas Park was regarded as "row upon row of cheap houses, sides bulging with children." One observer characterized Manassas Park as a "parasite."

Manassas and Manassas Park, in point of fact, *were* dissimilar. Manassas was an old community with a rich tradition and a relatively affluent population. Manassas Park was the new kid on the block. Much of the town consisted of bungalows built for GIs returning from World War II. As the cost of living in northern Virginia spiraled upward in the early seventies, Manassas Park becomes known as one of the few places where working-class families could afford to purchase a home.

Tensions between the two communities periodically erupted, as evidenced by a dispute in the early seventies over what to name the new high school to be shared by students from Manassas and Manassas Park as well as the boundary lines governing attendance at the school. Manassas Park officials complained that the Prince William County School Board favored Manassas residents on a variety of matters related to the new high school, including what to name it (Melton, 1998, p. 18). Relations were strained further when the town council of Manassas Park considered trying to annex Manassas.

Rebuffed in its efforts to negotiate a merger with its rival and aware of the impending state moratorium on the formation of new cities, council members in Manassas Park decided to take the steps necessary to make their town a city. Under Virginia law, a second-class city needed a population of at least five thousand. The 1970 census pegged the population of Manassas Park at 6,844, but a Prince William County planning document prepared in 1974 listed the population at 6,308 (Melton, 1998, p. 26). When the judge assigned to hear Manassas Park's petition balked because the town's population appeared to be declining, enumerators were hired to determine whether Manassas Park actually met the five thousand resident requirement. By mid-May they reported the population stood at 6,272. On May 15, fifteen days before the state moratorium on new cities was set to go into effect, the local circuit court judge signed the order establishing Manassas Park as a city. Two reasons were cited by the new city council for Manassas Park becoming a city (Melton, 1998, p. 27). First, Manassas Park students were at risk of being displaced as a result of Manassas becoming a city and forming its own school division. Second, Manassas's new status meant that its considerable tax base no longer would be available to benefit neighboring areas such as Manassas Park. While Manassas's revenues represented over one-tenth of the Prince William County tax base, Manassas Park's contribution to county coffers was a paltry 2.5 percent. Becoming a city would enable Manassas Park to raise its own revenue. On June 1, 1975, Manassas Park became the Old Dominion's newest city. What lay ahead for the infant city would test the mettle and resolve of residents and their representatives.

In no area of city government was the struggle to become an independent entity more daunting than public education. A hastily negotiated arrangement in the summer of 1975 enabled Manassas Park students for the time being to continue to attend Prince William County schools. Almost immediately, however, complaints were voiced about the amount of money Manassas Park was required to pay the county for educational services. The newly appointed three-person Manassas Park School Board sought advice from the Virginia School Boards Association about whether or not to form its own school division. Based on their shallow tax base, the school board was advised to continue paying tuition for students to attend Prince William schools (Melton, 1998, p. 28). It was reasoned that the cost of securing facilities to house its students would severely strain the new city's resources.

The school board attempted to negotiate a reasonable payment to Prince William County for educational services, but by April 1976, it was clear that no such deal was possible. County officials announced that educational services to Manassas Park students would be discontinued as of the fall of 1976.

Officials in Manassas Park now confronted the enormous task of planning a brand new school division in less than five months. A consultant was called in to examine facilities options and their costs. A number of public meetings were convened to discuss the development of a school system. These meetings invariably surfaced lingering concerns about the wisdom of leaving the Prince William County school

system. Other voices, however, contended that Manassas Park children
had not always been treated well in the county schools (Melton, 1998,
p. 32). When a second effort to negotiate an educational services agreement with Prince William County broke down, the Manassas Park City
School Board had no choice but to act. On May 27, 1976, board
members voted to launch their own school system in September. The
city council was asked to provide school buildings, equipment, and
funds to operate the system.

On September 15, 1976, a scant 111 days after, more than two
thousand Manassas Park young people entered their new city's schools
for the first time ("But They Did It," September 14, 1976, p. 4A).
Manassas Park had needed a miracle, and it got one. It would not be
the last time, however, that a miracle was called for.

In order to open for business in such a short period of time,
Manassas Park City Schools was compelled to contract for prefabricated
modularized buildings. City residents watched anxiously over the summer, uncertain until the doors opened on September 15 that construction actually would be completed on time. As it was, students and staff
members would have to wait for gymnasiums, libraries, and other special-
ized components. The recruitment and hiring of certified and classified
staff continued throughout the summer. In late June, the school board
chose Robert Strickland, an educator from Pineville, Kentucky, as the
school system's first superintendent (Leonard, June 25, 1976, p. 1). To say
that he had his work cut out for him is to risk serious understatement.

A PLETHORA OF POSTPARTUM PROBLEMS

The birth of a new school system is difficult under the best of circumstances. No one would argue, however, that Manassas Park enjoyed the
best of circumstances. No sooner did the school system come into
existence than it began to experience a bewildering array of internal
challenges. These included administrative turnover, school board tensions, inadequate resources, mismanagement, facilities problems, low
teacher morale, and disappointing student achievement.

Turmoil at the Top

When an organization experiences difficulties, it is only natural to look
first at its leadership. In the case of Manassas Park City Schools, every

time one looked, they were likely to find a change in school or division leaders. Administrative turnover constituted a persistent problem over the school system's first two decades. Melton (1998, p. 138) reported that between 1975 and 1995 MPCS had seven superintendents, twelve high school principals, fifteen high school assistant principals, seven middle school principals, nine principals at Conner Elementary School, seven principals at Manassas Park Elementary School, and eleven principals at Independence Elementary School. Trying to sustain continuity of mission under such circumstances was virtually impossible. It was hard enough just to keep track of who currently occupied key positions.

Manassas Park's first superintendent, Robert Strickland, suddenly submitted his resignation in April 1979 amidst a variety of complaints, ranging from the division's high dropout rate of 10 percent (one of the highest dropout rates in Virginia) to an exceptionally high student retention rate of 22 percent to the use of public funds for a trip to a Florida convention (Melton, 1998, p. 61). By the time Strickland's successor, Robert Lewis, took office, Manassas Park's enrollment had dropped to 1,747 students. Lewis lasted two years, departing in October 1981 for a superintendency in Louisiana. He left behind a school system with facilities in need of major repairs and two years of finances "in the red."

Gary Smith, a principal from a rural Tidewater school system, was next in the parade of superintendents. His tenure ran from January 1982 through March 1985 and was marked by continuing problems with facilities and criticism from city officials for lack of standardized policies and procedures. Smith was succeeded by Jimmy Stuart, who grappled with inadequate resources, annexation initiatives, school board turnover, enrollment growth, and low test scores during his three and a half years in office. Stuart refused reappointment by the school board when board members divided over his support for the principal of Manassas Park Intermediate School (School Board Minutes, Manassas Park City Schools, December 15, 1988). The principal had become the center of controversy when he implemented what some parents and students regarded as too severe a discipline system.

James Moyers became Manassas Park's fifth superintendent on July 1, 1989. Among the challenges confronting him were a persistently high dropout rate, teacher turnover of almost 25 percent, continuing problems with student achievement, and enrollment decline (Melton, 1998, p. 122). Moyers sensed that many students lacked the confidence to tackle rigorous academic work. He crafted a mission statement that focused squarely on the need to boost student self-esteem. To guide division improvement efforts, he won board approval for seven objectives, including the creation and enforcement of an effective student attendance policy, higher expectations for student achievement, better coordination of the instructional program across schools, and development of positive attitudes toward students by faculty and staff (School Board Minutes, Manassas Park City Schools, December 21, 1989).

Moyers appeared to possess insight into what needed to be done to steer Manassas Park out of its doldrums. Just as his efforts were beginning to yield results, however, he was diagnosed with pancreatic cancer. Forced to resign on January 16, 1991, because of failing health, James Moyers died twenty-one days later. Once again, Manassas Park City Schools was compelled to search for a new leader.

In some cases a lack of stable leadership at the top can be offset by strong leadership at the school level, but, as noted earlier, the turnover of principals and assistant principals was even greater than that of superintendents. Nor was the school board able to step into the breach and provide the necessary direction. Reports of deep divisions among board members surfaced soon after the creation of the new school system (Melton, 1998, p. 63). Relations among board members and between the school board and the educators of Manassas Park grew especially tense in 1983 when Grant Jones, the board's newest member, was chosen as chair. Jones questioned the need for special education teachers at his first board meeting, stating that too much money was being spent on students who were unlikely to be contributing members of society (School Board Minutes, Manassas Park City Schools, July 7, 1983). In the following months, Jones managed to alienate parents, community leaders, school system officials, and fellow board members (Melton, 1998, p. 89). By March 1, 1984, when Jones was pressured to resign by the city council and his fellow board members, he had meddled in administrative affairs normally handled by the superintendent, used his gavel to silence the legitimate concerns of parents and board members, attacked the mayor, and denounced teachers for petitioning for higher salaries.

While Jones's tenure as chair may have marked the school board's nadir, what followed could hardly be characterized as a golden age. Split votes were common, as was evidenced by the three to two vote to reappoint Superintendent Jimmy Stuart. After Stuart turned down the new contract and the school board hired James Moyers, several board members publicly criticized Stuart. Because Stuart was still the superintendent, the city council chastised the school board for acting unprofessionally (Melton, 1998, p. 120). More will be said later in the chapter about the perennially strained relations between the city council and the school board.

Given the divisions among board members for much of Manassas Park City Schools' infancy, it is easy to understand why the school system had difficulty attracting and retaining capable leaders. But board squabbles were only the tip of the iceberg. Below the surface lurked a variety of problems, the primary one being insufficient resources.

Education on the Cheap

Infants require adequate nourishment in order to grow to be healthy children. So malnourished was Manassas Park's new school system that many observers worried that it would not survive. In its first year of operation, Manassas Park City Schools spent $861 per pupil, based on its average daily membership (Annual Report, 1976–1977, p. 167). This amount was the lowest of any of Virginia's thirty-eight cities. Of the state's ninety-five county school systems, only rural Bland County spent less. Manassas Park's affluent neighbor, Manassas City, spent $1,336 per pupil, 35 percent more. Prince William County Public Schools, Manassas Park's previous educational host, allocated almost as much, $1,317 per pupil. Manassas Park's giant neighbor to the east, Fairfax County, backed each student to the tune of $1,607, while Falls Church, a small urban enclave surrounded by Fairfax County, topped the state with a $2,395 figure. Not only was Manassas Park deprived of resources, but it was surrounded by big spenders.

Succeeding years brought little improvement in the school system's fiscal circumstances. In 1980, when Manassas Park teachers pressed for a 17 percent pay increase, their division's salaries placed 115th out of 133 school systems in the state (Melton, 1998, p. 66). Not only did the teachers fail to receive such a substantial raise, but funds for a middle school remedial mathematics program were eliminated, despite the fact that 140 out of 160 eight graders qualified for remediation (Melton, 1998, p. 68). The city council did manage to find $57,530, however, to help build a new football stadium for the high school.

Lack of adequate resources doubtless was a factor in the high turnover rate among Manassas Park teachers and administrators. While such turnover spelled discontinuity for the division's educational program, it did mean that the school system could continue hiring first-year teachers, thereby keeping the budget relatively low. Over time, of course, the lack of experienced educators threatened to become extremely costly in terms of instructional effectiveness and staff leadership.

The school system's financial woes clearly were not of its own creation. No one who looked carefully at its salaries, bargain basement facilities, and primitive technology could ever accuse Manassas Park City Schools of squandering resources. Much of the division's fiscal difficulty derived from Manassas Park's tax rate, which, at $2.30 per $100 in 1981, was the highest in northern Virginia ("Call It Quits," October 21, 1981, p. A4). The high rate was due to the fact that 40 percent of the property in the city was owned by the city, thereby making it tax exempt. Put differently, those who owned the other 60 percent of the property had to carry the tax burden for the city. Lacking industry and large commercial firms, Manassas Park relied primarily on homeowners and small businesses for revenues. Understandably, the city council was reluctant to increase taxes.

Throughout the eighties, school officials prepared modest budgets, only to have them revised downward by the city council. No program or position was safe. At one point in 1986, the economic outlook was so bleak that consideration was given to consolidating the middle school and high school and eliminating athletics. Badly needed raises to enable the school system to recruit and retain qualified personnel and funds for capital improvements invariably got shifted to the back burner as school board and city council members struggled to make ends meet.

By the end of the eighties, hopes for a resolution of Manassas Park's perennial state of resource deprivation began to rise. After a twelve-year struggle with Prince William County, an agreement finally was reached in 1989 that allowed Manassas Park to annex 404 acres from the county. The annexation meant that the city would be able to develop several subdivisions, thereby expanding its tax base. The next few years proved disappointing, however, as school and city officials discovered that it takes more than available land for housing to generate additional revenue. As long as Manassas Park City Schools was perceived to be a low-performing school system, residential development was unlikely to take off.

Mismanagement and Investigations

Improving the public image of a school system is difficult when school officials regularly are accused of questionable practices. Within two years of opening its doors, Manassas Park City Schools found itself the focus of a parent-initiated investigation by the Virginia State Police (Melton, 1998, pp. 56–61). During the investigation, questions were raised about a variety of matters, including the lack of textbooks for students, and how money from school fundraising efforts was spent. Complaints were voiced by creditors who had not been paid in a timely manner. Investigators eventually discovered that Manassas Park's first superintendent had left his previous post in Lee County under a cloud of accusations regarding misappropriated funds (Melton, 1998, p. 59).

When Robert Strickland resigned as superintendent, the city took control of bookkeeping for the school system. In the fall of 1980, city officials discovered that Manassas Park City Schools was running a sizable deficit (School Board Minutes, Manassas Park City Schools, September 8, 1980). Superintendent Robert Lewis complained that it was impossible for his administrators to detect budget shortfalls when the budget was in the hands of city officials. Not only did the city council reject Lewis's request for budgetary control, but the city manager sought legal advice regarding possible code violations by the superintendent (Melton, 1998, p. 70). Lewis was told that any further deficits could result in legal action and possible removal from office.

Continued criticism of Manassas Park's superintendents inevitably cast a shadow on the school board that hired them and oversaw their actions. By 1984, city officials had reached the conclusion that much of their concern regarding mismanagement was due to a lack of adequate board policies and procedures. When a review of school board policies was conducted, a number of inconsistencies with Virginia law were found (School Board Minutes, Manassas Park City Schools, February 7, 1985). The school board contracted with the Virginia School Boards Association to bring Manassas Park's policies into line with state law.

Questions concerning school system leadership resurfaced at the end of 1988 when several school board members objected to Superintendent Stuart's support for the controversial principal of Manassas Park Intermediate School. After reassigning the principal to the central office, the school board voted to appoint an independent panel to investigate allegations against the principal of employee harassment, rude treatment of parents, and poor supervision of the special education program (Melton, 1998, p. 117). The panel was never constituted, but the reassigned principal resigned along with an intermediate school counselor who had been accused of sexual harassment.

Questionable Facilities

Investigations were not limited to school system leaders and policies. So worried about the status of the high school facility was Superintendent Lewis that he commissioned an architectural firm to conduct a thorough examination. The resulting confidential report somehow found its way to the local newspaper, which published parts of it (Curran, February 16, 1981, p. 1). There on the *Journal Messenger's* first page was the alarming statement that the high school's academic wings were "a potential fire bomb ready to go off at any time." The report indicated that the building was constructed of highly combustible materials, the fire warning systems were either nonexistent or inoperable, and the electrical panels were overheated.

The report generated considerable heat of its own. When Manassas Park's director of public safety called the state fire marshal's office to assist in inspecting the high school, other city officials went on the defensive, claiming that the report was intended to generate business for the consulting architect. One city council member went so far as to suggest that the intent behind the report was to move Manassas Park teenagers back to high schools in Prince William County (Melton, 1998, p. 73).

Besides concerns regarding fire safety, the report found that the hastily constructed modular pieces of the high school were settling unevenly and pulling away from the fire walls, creating roof leaks. The fire marshall for Manassas Park estimated that two million dollars would be required to shore up the problems, a figure far exceeding the $150,000 budgeted for maintaining school division facilities.

When the state fire marshal inspected the high school, he cited the school system for nine safety violations (School Board Minutes, Manassas Park City Schools, March 19, 1981). Two months later, it was discovered that the flooring in the high school was not strong enough to bear the weight of students. Required to bear eighty pounds per square foot, the high school's floors tested out at only forty pounds per square foot (Melton, 198, pp. 74–75). Action on correcting the problems was delayed as the school system unsuccessfully sought to acquire a facilities improvement loan from the state and then threatened a lawsuit against the company that constructed the school. Eventually a series of stopgap repairs were made to the high school, but no one believed that they would fully resolve Manassas Park's "edifice complex."

The annexation of land from Prince William County in 1988 again caused concerns to surface about Manassas Park's schools. A team of school officials constituted by the Virginia Department of Education was charged with surveying building needs in light of the annexation agreement and the anticipated enrollment growth associated with it. The team recommended thoroughly renovating Manassas Park's substandard facilities and building a new elementary and a new high school (Melton, 1998, p. 112). City officials expressed reservations, however, regarding the financing of these projects. It would take time, they reckoned, for the annexed land to be developed into tax-generating property.

Four years passed, and little progress was made on the facilities front. The school system asked VMDO, an architectural firm in Charlottesville, Virginia, to conduct a thorough investigation of Manassas Park schools. After his initial assessment, Robert Moje, the chief architect from VMDO, confirmed the school board's fears—Manassas Park's prefabricated facilities were in especially poor condition. Moisture from numerous leaks had accelerated the deterioration of the wooden structures, and the fire danger, despite efforts to correct it, remained alarmingly high. In light of these safety concerns and anticipated enrollment growth from annexation, Moje saw two options for the school board. Option one called for adding space to the existing elementary and high schools, renovating the original high school facility, and constructing a middle school and a second elementary school at new sites in the community. The second option involved building a new elementary and a new middle school on the same site as the high school and renovating the high school. The price tag for each option was close to twenty million dollars.

The school board and city council predictably supported different options. The school board preferred option two because of the logistical advantages offered by a single campus. Board members also reasoned that, since enrollment growth would be felt first at the elementary level, constructing a new elementary school should be the top priority. The city council, however, wanted to build a new high school first (Melton, 1998, p. 131). Council members also balked at the idea of a single K–12 campus and at the price tag for either option.

After months of squabbling, the school board and the city council finally reached an agreement on a capital improvement plan in May 1994. A new high school would be built on the fifty-nine-acre site of the existing high school. When the new high school was finished, the old high school would be renovated and converted to a middle school. The plan called for construction on the new high school to be completed by September 1999.

Morale Problems

Given all the issues regarding poor facilities, mismanagement, inadequate resources, tensions on the school board, and administrative turnover, it is not surprising that staff morale in MPCS was low. As noted earlier, Manassas Park teachers in 1980 pressed for a sizable salary increase, noting that their pay was among the lowest in Virginia. To make matters worse, class sizes routinely exceeded thirty students at the secondary level (Melton, 1998, p. 66). Despite a strong show of support for salary improvement by Manassas Park parents, the city council refused to consider any tax increase.

Teachers' hopes for salary improvement rose in the spring of 1983 when Governor Chuck Robb announced his support for higher salaries for teachers. Manassas Park received $240,000 from the state for salary increases, an amount that would have enabled the school division to boost pay by almost 10 percent. Rather than taking advantage of this opportunity to redress teacher grievances over pay, however, the city council instead used the largesse from the state to reduce its own contribution to the school system. As a result, teachers received a paltry 2 percent increase. Angered over this betrayal, teachers staged a "work-to-rule" protest by curtailing all commitments not specified in their contract.

By 1989 teacher frustrations over low salaries and lack of respect had reached a level where teachers began to openly criticize the school division. Some individuals expressed the view that Manassas Park should return to Prince William County or merge with neighboring Manassas

City (Turner, March 13, 1989, p. 1). To make matters worse, grievances were filed by teachers at the intermediate school regarding unprofessional treatment by the principal. A needs assessment commissioned by the school board and conducted in the fall of 1989 by the Center for Applied Research and Development at George Mason University revealed what most school system employees already knew all too well— teachers were often ashamed to admit they worked in Manassas Park, and they expressed very negative feelings about their conditions of employment (Center for Applied Research and Development, 1989). If additional proof of employee dissatisfaction was needed, one had only to consider the rate of staff turnover. The needs assessment reported that, of the 114 certificated staff members employed in September 1988, only 25 percent had been employed in June 1985!

Low Student Achievement

If Manassas Park students had performed well academically despite the adverse conditions previously described, it would have been miraculous. No such miracle occurred, however. In June 1980, the *Journal Messenger* (Curran, June 24, 1980, p. 1) reported that half of Manassas Park's eighth graders failed English and mathematics. Parents were so upset that they demanded that the superintendent be investigated. In the wake of the investigation, the high school principal resigned, citing philosophical differences with the central administration.

Achievement did not improve under new leadership at the high school. The students who struggled as eighth graders continued to struggle in the ninth grade (Curran, October 31, 1980). The problem was exacerbated because the new principal eliminated interim reports. Parents consequently had no advance warning that their ninth graders were in trouble academically. The new principal further upset parents when he changed the time for parent-teacher conferences from after school to regular school hours. As a result, many working parents were unable to meet with teachers and express their concerns.

Worries over low student performance continued throughout the eighties. Dissatisfied with student scores on the Iowa Tests of Basic Skills, the Manassas Park City Council convened a special meeting in October 1988 in order to grill school board members regarding the situation (Burns, October 25, 1988, p. 1). Flo Mullins, the school board chair, explained to the council members that low test scores reflected the school system's high rate of administrator and teacher turnover, the prevalence of new and inexperienced teachers, classroom management problems, and staff unfamiliarity with the tests. Council members were not persuaded by Mullins's remarks. They could not understand why Manassas Park students' test scores were the lowest in northern Virginia, on certain tests as much as forty percentile points below their neighbors in Prince William County and Manassas City (Melton, 1998, p. 114). One council member emphatically stated that the five-member school board should resign if scores did not improve.

Soon after James Moyers took over as superintendent of Manassas Park City Schools in July 1989, he visited all intermediate and high school English classes in order to hear what students had to say about their schooling. By this time Manassas Park's dropout rate was an alarming 8.5 percent (Melton, 1998, p. 122). Besides expressing resentment over having to attend schools in deplorable condition, the students complained that they were not challenged enough by their teachers.

SCHOOLING IN AN UNSUPPORTIVE ENVIRONMENT

It is difficult enough to launch a new school system, but when liftoff is impeded by local turbulence, the challenge becomes truly daunting. The environment in which Manassas Park City Schools found itself during its first two decades was anything but supportive. Manassas Park educators faced unrelenting criticism from parents and the press. The fledgling school division's greatest nemesis, however, turned out to be the city government.

Within months of the formation of MPCS, school board members were haggling with the city council over communications, purchase order processing, and even the type of flooring for the high school gymnasium (Melton, 1998, p. 40). The biggest issue, however, was money. In what would become a familiar complaint, the city council and the city administration were accused by school division administrators of failing to provide adequate resources to run an effective educational operation. Year after year, the budget process became a source of friction. Much of the problem was structural. Unlike many states, Virginia denies school boards the right to raise local revenue. As a result, educators must depend on the elected members of city councils and county boards of supervisors to provide the funds necessary to operate. While these elected officials are supposed to approve the overall amount of local revenue to which educators have access, they are not expected to meddle in decisions regarding how the funds are to be allocated. Manassas Park's council members apparently did not understand their role because, from the very outset of the school division, they insisted on being involved in managing the budget. Unlike other localities where school officials identified educational needs, constructed a pre-liminary budget, and negotiated the final allocation with the governing body, Manassas Park's "budget process" often consisted of the city coun-cil determining the amount of money the school division would re-ceive and presenting the figure to the school board as a fait accompli.

The Manassas Park City Council, from its inception, was aligned with a relatively conservative set of values. This alignment manifested itself in resistance to raising taxes and a reluctance to embrace higher salaries for school employees and funding for capital improvements. More than one superintendent left Manassas Park in frustration at the unwill-ingness of the city government to champion the cause of local education.

In the early eighties, city council and school board members battled over what to do with Connor Elementary School and the vacant Independence Elementary School. Interested in generating rev-enues, the city council proposed selling the Connor property, which was deemed to have commercial value, and reopening Independence, which was located in an area unlikely to attract real estate customers (Curran, April 16, 1982, p. 10). School board members were reluctant to close Connor unless they could refurbish Independence, which had been subjected to extensive vandalism. The issue became moot when the city council discovered how expensive it would be to move por-tions of the Connor facility to the Independence site.

By 1983 relations between the city council and the school system had deteriorated to the point where teachers, angry over their failure to obtain adequate raises, agreed to a "work-to-rule" job action. The city council countered with a public condemnation of the school sys-tem, claiming that it had drifted from teaching the basics, that the entire operation was disorganized, and that taxpayers were not getting their money's worth (Glier, June 15, 1983, p. 1). Furthermore, council mem-bers complained that too much emphasis was being placed on com-puter learning in the schools. Since the city council appointed individuals to the school board, council members threatened to express their displeasure by not reappointing uncooperative board members. They soon acted on their threat, opting to replace Kenneth Dellinger with Grant Jones, an attorney for the Internal Revenue Service whose only child was enrolled in a private school outside of Manassas Park (Melton, 1998, p. 88). On July 7, 1983, Jones was chosen to be the chair of the school board. Thus began a rancorous period when tension between the school board and the city council paled in comparison to quarrels among board members themselves.

Less than a year after Jones's appointment, the school board went into executive session to ask for the controversial chair's resignation. He was informed that this action was supported by the city council as well as the school board. No sooner had Jones stepped down, however, than the two governmental entities resumed their bickering. The budget, once again, was the main issue. The city council refused to accept the budget submitted by Superintendent Smith and insisted on a line-by-line accounting of all expenditures. The school board countered with a threat to meet the city council's demands for a reduced budget by cutting popular programs, including all athletics. When the school board returned its budget to the city council without having met the figure dictated by the latter body, council members decided to get even by voting five to one to reappoint Grant Jones to the school board (Melton, 1998, p. 97). Jones accepted the assignment, thereby reviving tensions within the school board and hastening Gary Smith's decision to leave Manassas Park.

A new superintendent, Jimmy Stuart, was appointed on April 1, 1985, but little else changed. School board members and city council representatives continued to disagree about the appropriate level of funding for the school system. When dismayed teachers threatened to find jobs in neighboring school divisions if their salaries were not raised, council members and Vice Mayor Donald Ticknor angered the teachers by declaring that Manassas Park teachers lacked the qualifications to land positions in a high-performing school system such as Fairfax County (Wren, April 5, 1985, p. 1).

When George Mason University's Center for Applied Research and Development conducted a needs assessment of Manassas Park City Schools in the fall of 1989, it found a school system suffering from a variety of problems, not the least of which was strained relations between the school board and city council. Strong and constructive leadership was prescribed. The source of such leadership, however, remained to be determined. Would it come from a dynamic superintendent, an assertive school board, or a reconstituted city council? The fact that members of the school board failed to agree on the validity of the commissioned needs assessment was not a hopeful sign. Nor was the city manager's decision in February 1990 to tell the school board how much funding they would receive before they had even prepared a budget!

Tensions between the school board and city council were not limited to finances. When capital improvements were debated in the early nineties, council members backed construction of a new high school, while board members preferred building a new elementary school. Perhaps the individuals chosen for the city council failed to understand their expected role vis-à-vis the school division. Manassas Park, after all, was a new governmental entity. Maybe the members of the city council were unaware that their charge did not include making decisions directly related to the educational program. Alternatively, the particular individuals elected to the city council may not have been disposed to trust educators to make appropriate decisions. Whatever the reason, one thing is clear. Over the first two decades of Manassas Park City Schools, the city council engaged in actions that can only be interpreted as micromanagement of matters normally left to the school board and its designees. That they were able to do so, often in spite of pressure from local parents, was due to the unusual arrangement under Virginia law whereby school divisions are unable to raise their own revenues or, at the time, elect their own board members. At least one observer found great irony in Manassas Park's circumstances.

> No matter how many parents we got to attend a meeting, or how prepared we were, we were always told [by the city council] that the majority of the taxpayers did not have school children and, as senior citizens, were on fixed incomes. Yet, the main reason we went to city status was because our children were short-changed in the county schools. Some "city fathers" apparently never saw the inconsistency in that! (Melton, 1998, p.134).

It is hard to imagine a school system in worse shape than Manassas Park City Schools in January 1991. Desperately short of resources, saddled with cheap and deteriorating facilities, plagued by contentious and even hostile relations between the school board and city council, and unable to achieve any semblance of academic success, the school division struggled to attract capable teachers and administrators. Low expectations and lack of confidence in the schools meant that many residents were reluctant to make the sacrifices necessary to improve Manassas Park's financial circumstances.

To put the school division's plight into more academic terms, what Manassas Park City Schools needed to do to ensure internal integration was undermined by the very steps it needed to take to adapt to its problematic external environment. In order to coexist with the city council, the school division had to settle for poor facilities, low salaries, the continuing prospect of underfunding, and constant meddling by elected officials in school business. These aspects of external adaptation predisposed the school division to high turnover, low morale, and political maneuvering, all of which contributed to internal fragmentation and organizational dysfunction.

To make a bad situation even worse, James Moyers, Manassas Park's promising new superintendent, was forced to leave office for health reasons early in 1991. The ship was adrift without a captain at the helm. Someone was desperately needed to arrest the downward spiral in which the school division found itself. When J. David Martin accepted the superintendency in April 1991, it finally looked as if Manassas Park had found the right person for the job.

CAUSE FOR HOPE

Martin did not take long to size up the situation. He recognized that the bottom line for a troubled school system was student achievement. Drawing on his background in Effective Schools principles, he focused attention on the improvement of instruction. Board member Frank Jones recalled that Martin's mantra was "all children can learn." According to Melton (1998, p. 128), Martin "promoted site-based management, teacher empowerment, and shared decision making, all strategies that he believed could take a profession and raise it to another level." Teachers were sent away to receive training in the instructional strategies of respected educator Madeline Hunter. Martin expected these individuals to return to Manassas Park and share their knowledge with colleagues. Those receiving training were reimbursed for their time. Excitement began to build among teachers and administrators. The new superintendent seemed to know how to get things done.

Martin next turned his attention to the deplorable condition of Manassas Park's schools. With school board support, he invited the architectural firm of VMDO to conduct a thorough examination of facilities. When Robert Moje, the architect heading up the study, reported on the serious nature of the division's facilities' problems and offered several options for correcting them, Martin got a taste of the political challenges that had faced his predecessors. The school board favored building a new elementary school first, reasoning that enrollment growth would be experienced initially at the lower grades. The city council, however, preferred starting with the construction of a new high school, an option that had not even been proposed by Moje. Martin and the school board eventually elected a pragmatic course, realizing that the city council controlled the purse strings. They began to explore the possibility of building a new high school on the site of the existing high school.

It had not taken Martin very long to learn about the political realities of schooling in Manassas Park. The real power in the school division resided with the city council. It took even less time for the new superintendent to discover that his own school board could be a source of concern. Soon after assuming his position, Martin asked that Lois Steele, the clerk of the school board, refer all calls from board members to him. According to Melton (1998, p. 128), Martin took this action in order to open up lines of communication between board members and himself. One board member, however, took exception to his instructions and, in an open session of the school board, accused Martin of withholding information from her. Frank Jones, a new board member, moved to go into executive session if personnel matters were going to be discussed. When the motion was seconded, the complaining board member walked out and did not return. Meeting with the press, she claimed her fellow board members had conspired to bully her into not disagreeing publicly with the new superintendent.

Martin also got a taste of parent discontent when Manassas Park agreed, as part of a regional commitment, to host a special education program at Independence Elementary School. The program, known as PACE (Positive Attitude and Commitment for Education), enrolled emotionally disturbed middle school students. Parents of kindergartners at Independence immediately expressed concerns regarding their children's proximity to potentially dangerous older students (Wolcott, November 1, 1994, p. 1). Martin was scolded for placing the safety of young students in jeopardy. When the local newspaper later published police reports on PACE students and their involvement in assaults at Independence, parents of young children at the school criticized Martin for concealing this information from them.

What had started out on such a promising note ended abruptly on March 11, 1995, when David Martin announced his resignation as superintendent. While Martin moved on to the superintendency of Henry County in the southern part of the state, Manassas Park City Schools once again found itself leaderless. Insiders reasoned that finding a capable person to head a school system that had gone through six superintendents in less than two decades would not be easy.

Chapter 3

An Improbable Choice
for an Impossible Job

If there is one universally acknowledged turning point in the history of Manassas Park City Schools, it is the selection of Tom DeBolt as superintendent. No knowledgeable gambler in 1995, however, would have wagered that DeBolt would be chosen to succeed David Martin. The most obvious reason was his lack of any central office experience. The highest position DeBolt had held prior to coming to Manassas Park was high school principal. So great a longshot was DeBolt that the person retained by the school board to handle the search for a super-intendent opted against including DeBolt's application in the collection of candidates forwarded to the school board for consideration.

How DeBolt came to be considered and eventually selected is a sufficiently incredible story to convince even the most skeptical observer that he and Manassas Park were destined for each other. DeBolt and Frank Jones, a board member at the time of the superintendent search, delight in recounting how Jones insisted on reviewing *all* thirty-seven applications, not just the ones that had been screened by the consulting headhunter. How Jones came to be on the school board in the first place is a story in itself. In fact, if DeBolt's coming to Manassas Park was the key to the school system's transformation, the key to the key was Jones's decision to get involved in his city's schools. This decision was prompted, Jones recalled, when he visited his son's elementary school and discovered that the flooring sank beneath his weight. Appalled that children were allowed to attend a school of such shoddy quality, Jones began to par-ticipate actively in the Parent Teacher Organization. Eventually he realized that the surest way to improve the schools was to gain a seat on the school board, which he proceeded to do.

When Jones read DeBolt's application, he spotted a familiar name. It was Leesville-Batesville High School in South Carolina. DeBolt had written in his resume that he consulted with Leesville-Batesville High School regarding the development of a 4 x 4 block schedule. As the principal of Pulaski High School in southwest Virginia, DeBolt had successfully implemented such a schedule and, in so doing, attracted the attention of University of Virginia professor and scheduling guru R. Lynn Canady. Canady began to recommend DeBolt as a consultant to schools interested in changing their schedules.

As fate would have it, Frank Jones had grown up in the Leesville-Batesville area, and several family members still resided there, one of whom worked at the high school. When he phoned his sister to inquire about DeBolt, she just happened to be with the high school principal and several faculty members. They all praised DeBolt for his work on the high school schedule and noted his interpersonal and staff development skills. As a result, the unlikely candidate was invited to meet with the Manassas Park School Board.

While DeBolt had never held a fulltime central office position, he was not lacking in educational experience or success. After stints teaching middle school in Dover, Delaware, and at the Peabody College Demonstration School in Nashville, Tennessee, he completed his doctorate at the George Peabody College for Teachers (Vanderbilt University) and accepted a position as assistant principal for curriculum and instruction at Parkway North Senior High School in Creve Coeur, Missouri. In 1975 he was appointed principal of James Monroe High School in Fredericksburg, Virginia, thus launching a twenty-year period as high school principal in four Virginia high schools. Along the way he was recognized as an outstanding principal by the Virginia Community Education Association, the National School Public Relations Association, the Virginia Association of Secondary School Principals, and the National Association of Secondary School Principals.

Landing a superintendent, of course, is a two-way process, and DeBolt was not certain that he and his wife wanted to abandon their beloved Blue Ridge Mountains and two-acre lakeside plot for the hustle and bustle of northern Virginia. That's when Frank Jones's talents as a salesman came into play. The retired Navy man and self-styled cheerleader for Manassas Park's young people took DeBolt on a personal tour of the city. Jones proudly pointed out where the new high school would go. His optimism about Manassas Park's future and his personal promise of support for the new superintendent finally persuaded DeBolt that he should take the job. And the rest, as they say, is history.

The chapter opens with a profile of Manassas Park City Schools in 1995 when DeBolt took the helm. The succeeding sections describe his efforts to secure adequate resources and make certain that that the new high school actually got built, efforts that required him to become politically active. The chapter concludes with the planning and completion of the new high school, which opened early in 1999.

THE CARDS DEBOLT WAS DEALT

Some new leaders expect to draw on new resources in order to effect change. Others must begin with what they have. DeBolt found himself in the second group when he took over as superintendent of Manassas Park City Schools on August 1, 1995.

Manassas Park served 1,561 students when DeBolt arrived. Of Virginia's thirty-six city school systems, only seven enrolled fewer students (*Superintendent's Annual Report for Virginia, 1995–96*, p. 2). The school system was listed as having 61.46 elementary teaching positions and 50.43 secondary teaching positions. The pupil/teacher ratio for elementary schools was eighteen to one, the second highest among city school systems in Virginia (*Superintendent's Annual Report for Virginia, 1995–96*, pp. 5–6). The pupil/teacher ratio for secondary schools, on the other hand, was 8.8 to one, third lowest among city school systems (pp. 5–6).

Data on the ethnic and racial make-up of the student body was not available for 1995, but in the fall of 1998, the first year for which such data was available, Manassas Park's student population consisted of 68.7 percent white (not Hispanic origin), 13.5 percent Hispanic, 13.6 percent African American, and 3.9 percent Asian/Pacific Islander. Almost 30 percent of the students were eligible for free or reduced price lunch, the primary index of student socioeconomic status.

The principal measures of student achievement across Virginia schools in 1995 were the Iowa Tests of Basic Skills. Designed to assess a student's status in the major skill and content areas, the Iowa Tests were administered in the fourth and eight grades. Table 3.1 contains the percentile scores for students from Manassas Park and Manassas City for the 1995–1996 school year. The percentile scores represent student performance as compared to students nationwide. A percentile score of thirty-seven, for example, means that the average score for Manassas Park fourth graders was higher than 37 percent of the national norm group of fourth graders. Table 3.1 indicates that Manassas Park fourth graders exceeded the fiftieth percentile only in science. Eighth graders performed somewhat better, though they never surpassed the fifty-eighth percentile. In no case did Manassas Park students perform better than their next-door neighbors, and the achievement gap between the two communities typically involved double digits. What was especially disturbing about the test scores of Manassas Park students was the fact that they were substantially lower than the previous year (Heisler, March 28, 1997, p. A-3).

High school students in Virginia in 1995 took the Test of Achievement and Proficiency (TAP) in the eleventh grade. Table 3.2 indicates the percentile scores for eleventh graders in Manassas Park and Manassas City for the 1995–1996 school year. While the gap between the two groups narrowed considerably, the level of performance in most cases was not especially high compared to the national norm. That Manassas Park students seemed to be performing better in high school must be viewed in light of the number of ninth graders who eventually graduated. Table 3.3 reveals that 58.8 percent of the 102 ninth graders in 1992–1993 went on to graduate in June of 1996. While some of the other 41.2 percent undoubtedly moved to other school systems and graduated, others dropped out of school. Assuming that many dropouts were low achievers, it is not surprising that the test scores of students who stuck it out and graduated would be relatively high compared to a school system with a lower dropout rate. That Manassas City graduated a larger percentage (74.6) of its ninth graders suggests that Manassas Park's neighbor held on to more students, an outcome that could have served to depress somewhat the school system's overall performance on the TAP.

Table 3.3 shows that 62 percent of Manassas Park students earned a Standard diploma, while over half (55 percent) of Manassas City graduates earned the more rigorous Advanced Studies diploma. Furthermore, half of Manassas City's 1995–1996 graduates went on to a four-year college (*Superintendent's Annual Report for Virginia, 1995–96*, p. 20). Only nine (15 percent) Manassas Park graduates attended a four-year college

Table 3.1. Percentile Scores for the 1995–1996 Iowa Tests of Basic Skills, Grades 4 and 8[1]

School Division	Vocabulary	Reading Comprehension	Language	Work-study	Math	Composite	Social Studies	Science
Grade 4								
Manassas City	65	67	76	72	72	73	70	76
Mannassas Park	37	38	35	45	42	40	41	62
Grade 8								
Manassas City	64	61	68	60	60	65	58	66
Mannassas Park	45	54	57	55	51	53	53	58

[1] *Superintendent's Annual Report for Virginia, 1995–96*, pp. 16–17.

Table 3.2. Grade 11: Test of Achievement and Proficiency, 1995–1996[1]

School Division	Reading Comprehension	Math	Written Expression	Sources of Info.	Social Studies	Science	Composite
Manassas City	54	57	67	66	61	70	61
Mannassas Park	55	47	58	55	61	60	55

[1] *Superintendent's Annual Report for Virginia, 1995–96,* p. 17.

Table 3.3. Graduation Data, 1995–1996[1]

School Division	Ninth grade membership for 1992–93	Standard Diploma 1995–96	Advanced Studies Diploma 1995–96	Special Diploma 1995–96	Certificate 1995–96	Total Grads 1995–96	%
Manassas City	382	122	158	3	2	285	74.6
Manmassas Park	102	37	16	7	0	60	58.8

[1]Superintendent's Annual Report for Virginia, 1995–96, p. 20.

immediately after graduation. Twenty-two other graduates (36.7 percent) enrolled in two-year colleges.

Another indicator of student performance is the annual promotion rate from one grade to another. For the 1995–1996 school year, Manassas Park promoted 91.3 percent of its students (*Superintendent's Annual Report for Virginia, 1995–96*, p. 8). Only six of Virginia's thirty-six urban school systems had lower promotion rates.

Manassas Park's new superintendent clearly had his work cut out for him with regard to student achievement. Many educators believe that it takes a substantial financial investment to turn around a low-performing school system. When DeBolt took over, Manassas Park's per pupil expenditure was 5,180 dollars (*Superintendent's Annual Report for Virginia, 1995–96*, p. 58.) This figure included local, state, and federal contributions. Of Virginia's thirty-six urban school systems, only eight spent less money per pupil than Manassas Park, and they were not located in northern Virginia where the cost of living was relatively high. Neighboring Manassas City's per-pupil expenditure was $5,623, $443 more than Manassas Park.

A primary reason for Manassas Park's low per-pupil expenditure was the relatively low value of property in the fledgling city. The *Superintendent's Annual Report for Virginia, 1995–96* pegged the true value of property in Manassas Park at $318,054,000 (p. 62). Manassas City, by comparison, had property valued at $2,033,389,000.

Lack of resources was reflected clearly in the average annual salary for Manassas Park teachers in 1995–1996. At $33,720, the figure for Manassas Park was lower than twenty-one of Virginia's thirty-six urban school systems (*Superintendent's Annual Report for Virginia, 1995–96*, p. 79). More importantly, Manassas Park's average annual salary was well below other school systems in northern Virginia, most of whose teachers averaged more than $40,000 a year. Competing for the best teachers under the circumstances was nearly impossible.

Manassas Park's relatively low levels of student achievement and resources certainly presented DeBolt with substantial challenges, but his greatest challenge could not be reduced to percentile scores or per-pupil expenditures. As he saw the situation in 1995, Manassas Park residents and those who worked for the school system shared a "damaged and defeatist institutional image." People lacked confidence that their schools could be improved. Teachers and administrators could hardly wait to leave. DeBolt characterized the school system as a "purgatory" that educators endured for as brief a period as possible until a better job in a more supportive environment could be found.

School board member Frank Jones vividly recalls the state of the school system when DeBolt arrived:

> In terms of facilities, we were clearly in need. We were not far from having to make some major declaratory judgments about the operating safety of some of our buildings. In terms of the staff and their professional competence, we were in need of some serious re-focusing and re-balance. It was the "do what you've always done, get what you've always gotten" problem. There was no understanding of how to improve the delivery of instruction.

Some communities might not have tolerated such conditions, but the residents of Manassas Park seemed resigned to having a mediocre school system. The year before DeBolt arrived, the state apparently made errors in calculating the amount of revenue due the school system. Frank Jones, the school board chair at the time, hoped that citizens would voice their displeasure and concern. Of the thousand or so families in Manassas Park, only fifteen people showed up at a public meeting devoted to the funding crisis. Jones bemoaned the "tremendous apathy" of Manassas Park residents (Keilman, February 17, 1994, p. 1A).

DELIVERING ON THE PROMISE

Faced with all the problems confronting his school system, Tom DeBolt might have been tempted to tackle them all simultaneously, a first act of leadership that probably would have been a finale as well. Instead, DeBolt sized up the situation and recognized that delivering on the school system's promise to build a new high school was job one. He knew that the successful completion of the high school could symbolize a new era for Manassas Park and serve as tangible proof that the school board with the support of Manassas Park residents and educators could accomplish something grand. He also knew that projected population growth made a new high school an absolute necessity.

DeBolt was savvy enough to realize that a high school planned is not a high school built. The journey from the drawing board to delivery of a finished facility was a circuitous one with plenty of opportunities for detours and disaster. Although the city council had approved a new high school prior to DeBolt's arrival, all the details concerning the financing of the project had not been worked out. A sudden downturn in the economy or change of heart on the part of key council members could substantially alter or even table plans for the new facility. DeBolt was well aware of his predecessors' continuous struggle for adequate resources to run the school system. Funding a new high school would require a major additional commitment on the part of Manassas Park taxpayers. So, while planning proceeded for the new high school, DeBolt busied himself mobilizing support for the project.

When DeBolt was working on his doctoral degree at Peabody, he recalled hearing that superintendents must scrupulously avoid partisan politics. Public education, his professors preached, should not be sullied by the deal making and tradeoffs that typically characterized local politics. It did not take long for DeBolt to realize that he would have to challenge this conventional wisdom in order to effect significant improvements in the education of Manassas Park students.

As DeBolt tells the story—a story that has become something of a local legend—he was intent on meeting as many people and making as many friends as possible when he first arrived in Manassas Park. Frank Jones, the school board chair, assisted him in getting to know the community. The two men quickly struck up a friendship that proved to be a critical element in Manassas Park's turnaround. DeBolt's efforts to win local support was bolstered by his and his wife's decision to buy a home in Manassas Park. His predecessors had opted in most cases to reside outside the city where upscale housing was more available. DeBolt's very tangible commitment to the community also meant that, if he chose to, he could become directly involved in local politics. He also joined the Lions Club in order to meet influential residents of Manassas Park.

For reasons that were unclear to both men, DeBolt and Jones were invited in May 1996 to attend the local Republican Party's "mass meeting" to pick candidates for the upcoming city council election. Despite being a "life-long Independent," DeBolt decided to attend. So did Jones. Only a handful of others attended. Three candidates were nominated, including an incumbent who was notorious for belittling and browbeating school system representatives when they petitioned the city council for funds. DeBolt described the trio as "regressives."

Realizing that whoever was nominated by the Republican Party stood a good chance of getting elected, DeBolt made up his mind to become involved politically. Despite their disdain for the city council's treatment of the school system, DeBolt and Jones supported the three Republican candidates. In doing so, DeBolt became a member of the Republican Party. Reflecting on this turning point in his superintendency, DeBolt noted that he grew up in South Chicago and was well aware of how local politics was conducted. The only way to change the makeup of the city council and thereby generate greater support for the school system was to work from within.

While his vision for Manassas Park Public Schools was yet to gel, DeBolt knew he could not effect a turnaround without the active support of the city council. When he returned from the "mass meeting," he discussed what lay ahead with his wife, Susan. They agreed that the city needed a new group of council members, individuals who cared as much for the young people of the community as they did about tax rates. Even though the next "mass meeting" was a year away, DeBolt and Jones were determined to find pro-education candidates to run for office and to mobilize as many education supporters as they could find to attend the May meeting. The result shocked the old-timers on the city council. Several "progressives," as DeBolt termed pro-education candidates, were nominated to run for city council.

Some leaders might have relied on political precedent and assumed that a Republican nominated was a Republican elected in Manassas Park. But Tom DeBolt was not just another leader. He took nothing for granted. He realized that one of the largest voting blocs in the city was the senior class at Manassas Park High School. They had the numbers, given the small size of Manassas Park and a light voter turnout, to sway a city council election. DeBolt also knew it was illegal and professionally irresponsible to coach seniors to vote for particular candidates. If the seniors only understood the issues and the platform on which each candidate was running, DeBolt was confident they were likely to support individuals who backed school improvements. In what has become a preelection ritual at Manassas Park High School, seniors attended a political forum where they learned about the positions of local candidates and how to participate in the voting process.

As a result of political activism on the part of DeBolt and Jones, the local political landscape in Manassas Park has changed dramatically. Within a few years, the makeup of the city council shifted from a group that viewed educators as adversaries to a team of pro-education supporters dedicated to working closely with the school board to develop a first-class school system.

When DeBolt arrived and assumed responsibility for the early planning of the high school, he could not be assured of unqualified support for the project. A year later, after joining with Frank Jones and others to rally local support, DeBolt calculated that he only could count on three of the seven members of the city council to press forward with actual construction. Two camps had emerged concerning the financing of the new high school. One group, which was strongly influenced by the city's financial adviser, Lawrence Wales, worried that Manassas Park faced a substantial long-term debt if it proceeded to build the high school while sales of lots in the city's new subdivisions lagged. This group preferred to slow down the project until the tax base grew.

The second group, represented most notably by Tom DeBolt and Frank Jones, argued that new families would be reluctant to buy lots and build in Manassas Park because of the poor condition of its schools. They advocated moving ahead with construction as quickly as possible in order to demonstrate to prospective buyers that the city was serious about improving its education system. As late as February 1997, the headline in the *Journal Messenger* reflected the prevailing uncertainty— "Many 'Ifs' Surround Manassas Park School" (Marino-Nachison, February 1, 1997, p. A5). The earliest completion date mentioned in the article was the fall of 1998, but the odds of opening a new high school by that time were considered slim.

Despite his growing support on the city council, DeBolt also was unlikely to receive the full amount he requested for construction. Knowing that construction costs would only rise with each passing year, DeBolt favored building a high school that would accommodate eight hundred students—the projected enrollment once the city subdivisions were built out—and a middle school at the same time. The estimate for this project was approximately twenty-eight million dollars. The city council offered thirteen million dollars, which would provide a high school for 650 students and no middle school.

DeBolt presented the city council with three options for the high school, each one in the neighborhood of thirteen million dollars, but varying in square footage and programmatic features. Plan A lacked an auditorium and a physical fitness center. Plan B included these features and ran about ninety-seven thousand square feet. Plan C, the one that DeBolt preferred, also included these features, but encompassed 101,000 square feet. At $14.2 million, it was the most costly of the three options, but it would mean that the students of Manassas Park would get a high school loaded with the latest technology. What there probably would not be room for, however, were traditional vocational classes. The city council committed, at least in principle, to the more expensive third option. DeBolt's political groundwork had begun to pay off.

Prior to the city council debating the details of financing the project and the best target date for completion, DeBolt had picked up where his predecessor left off and launched an extensive planning process. VMDO architect Bob Moje, who had conducted the aforementioned assessment of MPCS facilities, was retained to supervise the planning. He, in turn, engaged the KBD Planning Group of Bloomington, Indiana, to meet with local stakeholders, identify their desires for the new high school, and draw up a set of educational specifications. It is worth noting that many school systems at the time undertook planning new facilities without consulting parents, students, teachers, and school administrators. DeBolt realized, however, that if these stakeholders played a key role in the planning process and became excited about the new high school, they could put enormous pressure on the city council to support the project and expedite its completion.

ENVISIONING THE NEW HIGH SCHOOL

The fact that MPCS was a small school system with only one high school proved to be a great asset when it came to planning the new facility. Larger school systems with multiple high schools often face intense political pressure when a new high school must be built. Parents of students in existing high schools frown on the construction of fancy new facilities for other parents' children. As a consequence, large school systems often employ prototype designs and standardize their buildings. Those involved in planning the new Manassas Park High School were free, within the constraints of available funds, to imagine a truly innovative facility, one that would symbolize the beginning of a new era in the school system and the community.

The central figures in the planning process—Moje, DeBolt, and Bill and Kathy Day of the KBD Planning Group—were shrewd enough to realize that they were unlikely to extract a set of cutting edge design ideas from Manassas Park educators and citizens unless they engaged in some consciousness raising first. In other words, when people with little awareness of new developments in school design are asked what they would like in a school, they are apt to share relatively conventional ideas. Before engaging people in brainstorming possibilities for the new high school, DeBolt, Moje, and the Days made certain that a team of teachers from the middle school and high school visited examples of innovative facilities and learned about creative ways of designing learning environments. By doing so, the individuals who eventually sat down with the Days to develop a set of educational specifications had a wealth of interesting ideas to consider.

DeBolt's insistence on involving stakeholders in the initial planning of the new high school did not mean that he intended to keep his own thoughts to himself. DeBolt had done a great deal of thinking about what the new high school should look like and be like. First of all, his intention was to combine the middle school and the high school in one facility. DeBolt had visited Grafton Middle and High School in York County, Virginia, and been impressed with the cost effectiveness and utility of space sharing between the two schools. Grafton had two relatively independent academic complexes, one for the middle school and one for the high school, that were connected by an atrium housing a common cafeteria and media center and including a common gymnasium complex. Since both the middle school and the high school in Manassas Park needed to be replaced, DeBolt hoped to take advantage of the circumstances and get two schools for the price of one. He made certain that both middle and high school teachers participated in the planning process.

When it came to the educational program, DeBolt also had definite ideas. He wanted Manassas Park students to get a leg up on the competition by being exposed to the very latest in technology. Impressed by America's shift from a manufacturing to an information-based economy, he believed graduates of Manassas Park High School must be adept at communicating, problem solving, and interdisciplinary thinking. Rarely modest in his aspirations for young people, DeBolt noted in an interview on September 5, 1996, that "we're trying to create a Leonardo de Vinci . . . for the 21st century."

Educating latter-day da Vincis was unlikely, DeBolt believed, as long as teachers worked in isolation. The high school must cultivate interdisciplinary thinking by forging collaborative relations among teachers. Teamwork was the key. DeBolt was convinced, and Moje and his chief architect, Ken Thacker, concurred, that the physical design of a school could promote teamwork or inhibit it.

DeBolt even offered opinions about seemingly minor design details. He insisted, for example, that student restrooms should not contain mirrors. When mirrors are placed in restrooms, he argued, students spend too much time preening and then are late to class. Instead, mirrors should be placed in hallways and over water fountains. In this way, DeBolt believed students could quickly check how they looked without devoting inordinate time to the process.

The Days met on various occasions with middle and high school teachers and administrators as well as some community representatives and students to gather information on what people desired for the new facility. Stakeholders were asked about what they wanted Manassas Park students to learn, how they wanted learning to occur, and the settings in which learning should take place. The Days, along with Moje, Thacker, and DeBolt, were convinced that the effectiveness of learning and teaching is inextricably linked to the quality of the physical space in which it takes place. By May 1996, the Days had sufficient input to develop a set of educational specifications and submit them to DeBolt and the school board for consideration.

The document opened with a future-oriented vision statement that clearly indicated Manassas Park's intention to create a high school focused on tomorrow's needs, not today's. The executive summary condensed the vision statement thusly:

> The winds of change are sweeping across this country as educational leaders, planners, and architects seek a new vision in redefining America's high schools. We must prepare for the global community in which we will live, prepare young people that are creative, productive thinkers, motivated, compassionate, responsible, and flexible individuals. We

can do more to mold a quality producer, an effective team
member, a competent communicator, and positive contribu-
tor to our country. ("Educational Specifications . . . ," May
1996, p. 1)

In order to realize this ambitious vision, the educational
specifications called for six key elements: (1) interdisciplinary teams, (2)
block scheduling, (3) an organizational structure subdivided into small
units, (4) widespread use of technology, (5) a facility capable of serving
as a community center, and (6) a student commons.

Interdisciplinary teams were premised on the belief that productive problem solving in the real world necessitated thinking across
academic specializations. Students were not apt to appreciate the value
of interdisciplinarity if their teachers were not organized in ways that
promoted cross-fertilization. The specifications consequently called for
teachers to be organized and housed in interdisciplinary groups. Teams
of teachers from different academic areas would share work space, meet
and plan together, and model interdisciplinary thinking for students.

Instead of the traditional seven or eight-period day in which
students switched classes every forty to forty-five minutes, the
specifications envisioned a block schedule divided into "A" and "B"
days. Students would take four classes, each one and a half hours in
length, on the "A" day and a different four classes of the same duration
on the "B" day. Longer class periods and fewer classes per day promised
greater teacher-student interaction and more opportunity for uninterrupted classroom activities. In addition, less time each day would be
wasted moving from class to class, a benefit that also had implications
for school discipline, since many behavior problems occur during passing time between classes.

Designing a high school around small learning communities was
intended to foster greater teacher familiarity with students and their
learning needs. Students, it was believed, would be more likely to
develop constructive relationships with teachers if they were organized
into discrete clusters or houses.

Participants in the planning of the new school felt strongly that
access to the latest technology was crucial if Manassas Park students
were to hold their own against their peers in more privileged school
systems. The specifications indicated that students should be trained to

use the same "personal productivity tools" used by adults in the work-place. DeBolt envisioned a facility where students could plug in their laptops wherever they decided to settle and study.

Building a new school in a relatively poor community such as Manassas Park requires considerable sacrifice on the part of local taxpay-ers. Understanding this fact led planners to insist that the new facility should also serve as a resource for adults in the community. The weight room, for example, should double as a "fitness center" available to adults after school. The specifications also recognized the need for partnerships between the new high school and local businesses and agencies.

The sixth component of the specifications addressed the value of "gathering spaces" for students. A high school should not be a place of incarceration, but instead a comfortable environment that welcomes young people. There would be a student commons that also served as an eating and entertainment center. As the specifications put it, "The new high school for Manassas Park will be like a good house, for students and teachers, in that it will have a variety of spaces that provide a variety of opportunities for interaction" ("Educational Specifications . . . ," May 1996, p. 2).

When the educational specifications finally were presented to the community, one anticipated feature was missing, and its absence con-stituted the only major disappointment of the planning process for DeBolt. The specifications lacked any reference to a combined middle and high school. The estimated twenty-three million dollar price tag was simply too high for the city council to accept, based on existing revenues. Even the $14.2 million figure to which the city council agreed would be a stretch for the cash-strapped city. When asked whether he had any regrets about the process of planning the new high school, DeBolt acknowledged that he was sorry that the hopes of middle school faculty and parents of middle schoolers had been raised prema-turely. They would have to wait for their new facility and, at the time, no one could predict when the city would have sufficient funds to undertake such a project.

Tom DeBolt is indisputably an idealist, but he is a realistic idealist. He realized that there was nothing to be gained by digging in his heels and insisting that the city council find the funds to construct a com-bined middle and high school facility. He instead banked on the ripple effect of completing the new high school. If the project turned out as he hoped, momentum would build for other capital improvements. He also counted on getting more "progressives" elected to the city council so that when he returned with a new request for funds, he could count on political support. It was now up to the architects at VMDO to draw on the educational specifications and deliver a "world class" facility to accommodate up to 650 Manassas Park high school students.

FROM BRAINSTORMING TO BRICKS

Working over the summer of 1996, Bob Moje, Ken Thacker, and their colleagues at VMDO sought to translate the "dreams" for the new high school into a design. By August 24, the *Manassas Journal Messenger* was able to run a story featuring the initial layout for the facility (Marino-Nachison, August 24, 1996, p. A1). The three-story building was shaped like the letter L, with each side of equal length. On the inside where the two wings met was the signature design feature—a three-story circular structure, or drum, on the first floor of which was the student commons. Circling this open space on the second floor of the drum was the media center. DeBolt and the architects felt strongly that the school's focal point should be a feature other than the gymnasium, the typical focus of attention for many highs schools. They contended that a high school should be, first and foremost, a meeting place for students and an academic enterprise. Having the student commons and media center at the new school's "heart" sent the right message.

The design called for all of the "noisy" and movement-oriented activities to be located on the first floor, leaving the second and third floors for classrooms and science labs where quiet was preferable. At both ends of the second floor were located business and computer labs. Connecting the second and third floors on each wing of the L were wide carpeted stairs on which students could gather for conversation and mini-classes. In the middle of these stairs was located another unique feature of the school—a two-story teacher workroom complex with windows looking out on the stairs and the adjacent student restrooms. This arrangement ensured unobtrusive student supervision by teachers working in the workrooms. The first floor was occupied by the administrative and guidance offices, the band and chorus rooms, and the visual arts room (which was blessed with ample natural light and looked out on the heavily wooded rear of the school), the pottery studio, the school store (which also served as the marketing lab), and the student commons (which doubled as the food court and auditorium). At one end of the L, where the new high school joined the old gymnasium complex, a fitness center and weight room was located.

In order to save money in the future, when the high school would need to expand to accommodate residents of the developing subdivisions, the architects made certain that the student commons, media center, and gymnasium complex were built for a school of eight hundred students. The mechanical systems also were designed to accommodate eventual growth. When the time came for the high school to grow, only classrooms would need to be added.

The new high school would be linked to the old high school, which would become the middle school, by the gymnasium complex, creating in a single visual image a picture of where Manassas Park City Schools had been and where it was headed. Once students and staff members saw the design, they could hardly wait for construction to be completed. DeBolt knew, however, that between the blueprints and the final bricks lay a considerable amount of maneuvering and arm-twisting. The mayor, Ernest Evans, was yet to be convinced that the city could afford the impressive facility presented by VMDO and praised by DeBolt. There were calls for scaled-down versions. DeBolt was convinced, however, that only an impressive facility would attract residents to Manassas Park's new subdivisions and, with them, new revenues for city coffers. As he put it, "You have to make a leap of faith. If we build it, they will come." Meeting with the mayor at his home, DeBolt persuaded him to support the VMDO design. Evans expected DeBolt to do whatever he could to keep costs down. Construction was scheduled to begin in July 1997. A great believer in the symbolic value of ceremony, DeBolt scheduled a community groundbreaking on the Fourth of July to launch the project.

Two crucial decisions were made that enabled DeBolt to fulfill his promise to Evans and keep the project within budget. The first decision was made when the school board agreed that the school system would serve as the general contractor for the new high school. The school board hired a Maryland-based construction management firm to oversee the work of nearly thirty separate contractors, ranging from an excavation outfit to a drywall firm (Meixner, October 30, 1997, p. A1). As the school system's agent, the construction management firm also was expected to effect savings wherever possible. Manassas Park thus became one of the first school systems in Virginia to elect the construction management alternative.

The second decision involved a spending and accounting process DeBolt referred to as "positive arbitrage." By following a carefully orchestrated spending schedule dictated by the Internal Revenue Service, which in many cases called for purchasing materials well before they were needed just to ensure that a certain level of expenditure was maintained, the school system significantly reduced its costs. Mayor Evans's support for the more expensive high school design, in fact, was premised on the $250,000 in savings DeBolt promised from positive arbitrage. To implement the process, the city council had to vote every month for eighteen months on what funds to appropriate for construction and whether to continue with the project. At no time during construction did DeBolt and the school board enjoy the certainty of knowing that the high school would be completed on schedule. Every month's vote in the city council created an opportunity for anxieties to be raised about revenues and design details.

To maintain interest in the project during construction, the high school principal, Margaret Huckaby, got students to don hardhats and tour the building. She knew that the more excited students got about the new school, the harder it would be for the city council to back off its commitment or slow down the timetable for completion.

Before the last brick was laid at the new facility, DeBolt would learn a hard lesson about tradeoffs and the political process. Concerned about the assumed debt associated with building the high school, city officials ordered almost a million dollars cut from the school system's proposed operating budget for 1998–1999 (Meixner, January 7, 1998, pp. A1, A3). While some of the money eventually was reinstated, the school system's budgets for 1998–1999 and the following year were less than requested. It would take several years before sales of lots in the new subdivisions generated enough revenue to allay the city council's fiscal concerns.

On February 14, 1999, the city of Manassas Park got a unique Valentine—a gleaming new high school that would go on to win design awards and achieve national recognition. To mark the occasion, DeBolt and the school board invited the community to participate in moving furniture, files, and equipment from the old facility to the new building. The day took on the character of an Amish barn raising with students, parents, community members, educators, and members of the architectural team working shoulder to shoulder to ready "the home of the Cougars" for its first day of instruction.

Manassas Park residents got much more than a well-built, state-of-the-art place in which to educate their teenagers on Valentine's Day. As a turning point in the history of Manassas Park City Schools, the opening of the new high school was second only to DeBolt's selection as superintendent. The high school almost immediately came to symbolize the beginning of a new era in the history of Manassas Park. No longer would student athletes be embarrassed to host their peers from other high schools. Taxpayers had made a sacrifice, but a sacrifice of the most worthy kind—a sacrifice to benefit future generations. The new high school was proof positive that the fledgling school system could achieve something big and do so efficiently, on schedule, and without accusations of mismanagement. Manassas Park now possessed a concrete symbol of its commitment to young people and a visible focus for community pride. The coming years would determine whether the learning that took place within the new high school would match the hopes that had begun to grow.

RAISING ACHIEVEMENT IN AN
ERA OF ACCOUNTABILITY

Manassas Park High School would have faced a significant challenge if it had had to boost student achievement based on the expectations that students had faced during the school system's first two decades. By the time the new high school opened, however, the ante had been raised. The Commonwealth of Virginia, responding to widespread pressure for greater educational accountability and improved student achievement, adopted a new set of Standards of Learning in mathematics, science, and language arts on June 22, 1995 (Duke & Reck, 2003). The Standards of Learning were destined to become the basis for state standardized tests to be administered to students in third, fifth, and eighth grade as well as high school. Testing was set to begin in the spring of 1998. Students who failed the tests would face retention and, ultimately, the prospect of not graduating. Besides state standards and tests aligned to the standards, Virginia's tough educational accountability program included revised Standards of Accreditation that included warnings for schools not achieving prescribed pass rates on state tests. To ensure public awareness of school performance, the accountability program also called for School Performance Report Cards to be sent to parents and the media. If a school failed to meet state standards, it would have no place to hide.

A year before the new high school opened, the school board sent Manassas Park parents a booklet explaining Virginia's new standards (Bhagwandin, January 26, 1998, p. A1). The message was clear: promotion henceforth would be tied to performance, not age. Ambivalence toward the new state educational accountability program surfaced almost immediately and was captured by the following newspaper quote from a Manassas Park parent:

> It's great for students who want a college education, but the majority of the students from Manassas Park do not go on to college. The standards are so rigid and the students won't be able to take vocational classes, because they will have to concentrate in the core subjects . . . (Bhagwandin, January 26, 1998, p. A5)

The parent's comment proved prescient when a month later DeBolt announced that Manassas Park would cut vocational programs in cosmetology and automotive mechanics (Bhagwandin, February 19, 1998, p. A2). Despite the protests of many parents, the school board voted four to one to support the decision. In defending his action, DeBolt said that the vocational teaching positions had been cut in order to give students greater opportunity to focus on the core subjects—English, math, science, and history (Bhagwandin, March 5, 1998, p. A1). He went on to point out that Manassas Park students' test scores were generally low and they would need "extra help" in order to pass the new state tests. Nothing was said at the time about the lack of assigned space for vocational classes in the soon-to-be-opened high school. There would be no mistaking the new focus on academics in Manassas Park City Schools. Manassas Park might be a working-class community, but its young people were going to have the opportunity to go to college if Tom DeBolt and the school board had anything to say about it.

Another action taken prior to opening the new high school that sent a clear message regarding the direction in which Manassas Park

City Schools was heading involved Ben Kaiser, the high school principal who preceded Margaret Huckaby. Knowing that he was being promoted to the role of assistant superintendent, Kaiser, just prior to handing over the reins to Huckaby, refused to recommend a number of high school teachers for continued employment. DeBolt recalled that there were "eight or nine teachers, mostly nontenured, who were extremely negative." These individuals resented staff development, disliked being asked to devote part of their summer to improving their teaching, and balked at requests to become more proficient with the use of computers in the classroom. Looking back, DeBolt felt that Kaiser could not have done his replacement a greater favor than dismissing this group, what amounted to almost one-quarter of the high school faculty. His initiative allowed Huckaby to avoid being labeled a "hatchet man" and freed her to hire individuals who were committed to building a top-notch high school.

Whether the new academic emphasis coupled with opening the new high school and bringing new teachers on board played an immediate role in raising student achievement may be impossible to prove, but one thing is clear. When Manassas Park City Schools received the results of state testing in the spring of 1999, high school students' scores rose in every tested subject (Bhagwandin, July 30, 1999, p. A1). Algebra, which had been a subject where earlier scores had been particularly low, experienced a 33 percent jump in passing scores.

While pleased with the progress, DeBolt was the first person to admit that any celebrations would be premature. Despite improved test scores, no Manassas Park school in 1999 would have had enough students passing the tests to meet the state's accreditation standards, had they been in effect. The state standards set the benchmark for the number of students passing state tests at 70 percent. Virginia's new program would be used for the first time in 2004 to determine which students were qualified to graduate with a state diploma. Manassas Park therefore had several years to work on raising student performance. With the new high school completed, some of this effort now would be directed at improvements in the education of elementary students. DeBolt believed that one of the first steps in this direction had to be construction of a new elementary school.

Chapter 4

Excellence Begins Early

Construction on the new high school had barely begun when Tom DeBolt and the school board shifted attention to planning a new elementary school to handle Manassas Park's youngest students, those in kindergarten and grades one through three. The elementary school project had been their preferred starting point for capital improvements, but the city council held out for launching the new high school first. Several observers confided that they felt the city council's decision had been influenced by the fact that several council members' children were enrolled in or scheduled to attend the high school.

DeBolt and the school board had reasoned that Manassas Park's population growth first would be felt at the elementary level. Between 1993 and 1998, the number of students attending Manassas Park schools climbed from 1,386 to 1,710, a 23 percent increase (Bhagwandin, September 15, 1998, p. A1). DeBolt was quoted in the *Manassas Journal Messenger* as estimating that the elementary-age population would double by 2001, assuming the new subdivisions filled.

In 1998 Manassas Park operated three elementary facilities: Independence Elementary School for kindergartners, Manassas Park Elementary School for grades one through three, and Conner Elementary School for grades four through six. A full-day kindergarten program had been implemented for the first time at Independence. Independence and Conner were in particularly poor condition and needed replacement as soon as possible. Overcrowding also had begun to take its toll, as twelve modular units were placed on two of the three sites. Manassas Park Elementary, the best of the three schools in terms of quality, was forty years old. DeBolt made no secret of his feelings. "We

55

can't build a new school fast enough," he told a reporter (Bhagwandin, September 15, 1998, p. A1). What he did not share with the media was his belief that the academic program for elementary students also needed some quick improvements.

DeBolt hoped that the success of the new full-day kindergarten program would be experienced in the other elementary grades. In just its first year of operation, the full-day kindergarten was credited with a dramatic increase in the percentage of kindergartners entering first grade at average or above average levels in the skills needed to be good emergent readers and writers. In the alphabet recognition test, for example, twenty-two students had scored at the lowest level and eight students at the top level before the introduction of full-day kindergarten. After the first year of full-day kindergarten, only one student scored at the lowest level and fifty-five students scored at the highest level. The first step toward academic improvements for other elementary students, in DeBolt's mind, was better facilities. He reasoned that a new school could be the impetus for across-the-board changes in teaching and learning.

The chapter opens with a discussion of several sources of controversy concerning the construction of a new elementary school. Contentious issues included the school's location and funding. Subsequent sections describe the planning, design, and completion of the facility. The chapter concludes with a discussion of the impact of the new school and its academic program on student performance.

WHERE WILL IT BE AND CAN WE AFFORD IT?

Deciding where to locate a new school can be a difficult process, especially in a small city with a growing pattern of social stratification. Placing a new school in a particular neighborhood can be a vote of confidence in that part of the community. Deciding not to place a new school in a particular neighborhood is a non-act of great symbolic importance as well. New residents and commerce frequently follow new construction. New schools, in other words, are good for business.

By the time Tom DeBolt and the school board turned their attention to the location of a new elementary school, Manassas Park consisted of two distinct residential areas—the older neighborhoods, which contained postwar bungalows and less up-to-date housing, and the new subdivisions with relatively expensive homes in the area annexed from Prince William County. After four possible school sites were evaluated, the school board agreed that the site best suited for the new school was located on Brandon Street in Blooms Crossing, one of the new subdivisions. One influential member of the city council continued to insist that the new school should be located in the older part of Manassas Park, but the site that he preferred, along with several others, was rejected as being too small and topographically unacceptable. Another council member complained that the twenty-five-acre Blooms Crossing site had substantial commercial value and should not be designated for public use (Daugherty, November 13, 1998, p. A3). By the time these reservations were expressed, DeBolt and his allies had four votes on the seven-member city council, thereby assuring that the new school would be built in the new section of the city. That was where the growth was, supporters reasoned. DeBolt, whose home was adjacent to the preferred site and who was becoming something of an architecture buff, would be able to monitor every phase of construction from his backyard. That is, if the money could be found to build the new school.

While there were murmurs of disapproval from some quarters regarding the new school's location, there was open resistance to incurring more debt on the heels of the new high school project. For half a year from the summer of 1998 to the early spring of 1999, DeBolt rode a roller coaster of expectations concerning funding for the new elementary school. At least one member of the city council went on record early as opposing the new school (Anderson, September 10, 1998, p. A1). In January 1999, Lawrence Wales, the financial advisor who had cautioned against building the new high school, suggested that the city council put the elementary school project on hold (Bhagwandin, January 14, 1999, p. A3). DeBolt challenged Wales's recommendation, pointing out that his advice previously had missed the mark.

Prospects for the new elementary school were not looking good on January 18, 1999, when the *Manassas Journal Messenger* ran the following headline: "New Manassas Park School Not High on Budget Priorities." An estimated $8.5 million to enable the school system to begin construction on the $14.5 million project had not been entered as a line item for Manassas Park's 1999 fiscal budget (Bhagwandin, January 18, 1999, p. A1). The city's planning commission, which classified all capital projects as either "urgent," "necessary," or "desirable," had given the elementary school a "necessary" rating. As a rule, only projects labeled "urgent" earned a line item in the budget. DeBolt suffered another setback when a school board member publicly announced opposition to the project.

March, however, brought encouraging news that the school board unanimously passed DeBolt's $13.2 million budget ("News Brief," March 5, 1999, p. A3). The budget included funds for thirteen new teaching positions and a 6.25 percent across-the-board pay increase. The city council, which was slated to pick up $4.6 million of the school system budget even agreed to add an extra one hundred thousand dollars for new athletic uniforms and a school bus. Funding for the new elementary school, however, remained uncertain.

The key to financing the project involved Manassas Park's bond rating, which determined the rate of interest on city bonds and ultimately how much money could be borrowed to begin construction. Saddled with a "less-than-favorable" bond rating in the past, Manassas Park received an upgraded rating in March 1999 (Anderson, March 19, 1999, p. A3). The timing could not have been better for DeBolt. City officials planned to seek approval for a bond in April in order to pay for the new high school. If the new bond rating allowed the city to secure a lower interest rate for the high school bond, city council members would be more likely to support a second bond for the elementary school. It did not hurt that economic conditions in Manassas Park were steadily improving. In January, for example, city residents learned that Manassas Park had the lowest unemployment rate in the state—one percent. The city had started out the previous year ranked fifty-fourth in Virginia (Anderson, January 14, 1999, p. A3). Thanks to a booming economy in northern Virginia, Manassas Park actually found itself running a budget surplus.

By December 2000, the city council had reason to feel flush, what with a two million dollar surplus and low local unemployment. The local newspaper opened an article on Manassas Park's rising circumstances with the following statement: "Gone are the tough financial times of the last decade when city funds were short, police cars were breaking down, and city workers had to be laid off" (Newman, December 1, 2000, p. A3). The article went on to explain that the turnabout in city finances was due largely to the increased tax base created by the sale of homes in Blooms Crossing and other new subdivisions. Tom DeBolt could not help smiling over the correctness of his prediction— "If we build a new high school, they will come." Even more would come, he suspected, when the new elementary school was completed.

PLANNING THE NEW ELEMENTARY SCHOOL

Tom DeBolt is not the kind of leader who waits until project funding is assured before commencing the planning process. There are risks, of course, in moving too quickly, as he learned when he was forced to tell a disappointed middle school faculty that money for a combined high school and middle school was unavailable. But there also are risks with an overly cautious approach to change. Had DeBolt not initiated planning for the new elementary school in 1998, prior to securing funding for the project, the school system most likely would have been unprepared to commence construction soon after getting the news of the bond rating upgrade and subsequent approval of funding for the project. A delay, in hindsight, could have been disastrous, given the bursting of the high technology bubble in 2001 and the post-9/11 plummet in the economy. Trying to get a new school built under such trying circumstances might have been nearly impossible. Instead, Manassas Park opened its new elementary school just as the first signs of a slowing economy were being detected.

Pleased with VMDO's work on the high school, DeBolt and the school board again turned to the Charlottesville architectural firm to help plan and design the new elementary school. VMDO president Bob Moje enlisted William Bradley, a recently hired specialist in school planning, to assist in the process. Bradley had a doctorate in education and a bachelor's degree in architecture. Prior to joining VMDO, he had been assistant director of the Thomas Jefferson Center for Educational Design at the University of Virginia, an organization devoted to exploring new ways to design learning environments. Moje and Bradley engaged the services of the director of the Jefferson Center in order to raise awareness of organizational alternatives for a large elementary school. They also invited a professor from James Madison University to provide expert advice on elementary school scheduling. Moje and Bradley realized that how a school was organized and how students were scheduled for instruction were inextricably related to the school's physical design. Waiting until after the school was built to discuss the daily schedule made little sense, since the availability of classroom space would determine how many students could be accommodated for particular types of instruction at designated points in the day. Knowing in advance how the school would be subdivided and the grade levels arranged would help designers allocate space in ways that complemented the educational program.

The VMDO planning team spent several months working with Manassas Park Elementary School teachers and administrators to develop a basis for the new school's educational specifications. DeBolt made it clear to the planning team that he viewed the development of a new elementary school as an opportunity to rethink the entire program, kindergarten through third grade. He had no intention of building an impressive new facility to house an old and not particularly effective educational program. All that was certain regarding the new school was that it needed to be large enough to accommodate at least one thousand students.

Given the size of the new school, the VMDO and school-based planners knew that the design would have to include provisions for the needs of very young children, possibly including prekindergarten-age youngsters. A facility for one thousand or more students easily could overwhelm and intimidate. One way to reduce the impact of school size that was explored by the director of the Jefferson Center was to subdivide the school into smaller segments or houses. This arrangement was popular in middle and high schools, but had not been tried extensively at the elementary level. Various bases for subdividing the school were identified and critiqued. Houses, for example, could be organized horizontally by each grade level or vertically to include all grade levels. Other possibilities included grouping students by instructional philosophy or content area. At one point, a three-house arrangement was examined, with one house devoted to traditional self-contained classes, another house reserved for teachers who looped (followed their class from one grade level to another), and a third house that focused on some innovative instructional approach or departmentalization by subject areas. Whatever the basis for subdividing the school, all agreed that three freestanding and interconnected houses, each designed for approximately three hundred students, fit very well with the type of structure that had to be built on the available property. The school needed to have three stories in order to accommodate all the early-elementary-age students in the school system. It was hoped that the new facility also would include a separate prekindergarten complex for one hundred youngsters.

Creating a large elementary school with multiple stories and subdividing it into houses challenged assumptions about how to design and organize an elementary school, especially one for the very youngest students. The planners did not stop here, however. Another assumption that was challenged early in the process was that young children needed to be taught in self-contained classes. Moje and Bradley used a "framing question" to stimulate innovative thinking: "What if elementary students did not spend all day in the same classroom?" Teachers and administrators began to consider the possible benefits of exposing young students to different teachers and different settings during the school day. They questioned the conventional wisdom that held that most children would not function well if they had to negotiate different classes with different teachers and different sets of expectations. Evidence to support this traditional belief turned out to be in short supply, so planners entertained the possibility that the quality of instruction actually might be enhanced if students were exposed to several specialists in addition to their homeroom teacher. Eventually, the planners proposed that students would study reading and mathematics with their homeroom teachers and then move to specially equipped "centers" to study social studies, science, and technology. Each center would be hosted by a specialist in the content area.

One of the consultants noted that some form of parallel block schedule would be ideal for this arrangement, often referred to as departmentalization. With students moving into and out of their homerooms during the school day, it would be possible to group students in different ways for instruction. Students, for instance, who needed more assistance with reading, might receive additional help in a small group while other students worked in one of the centers. Elementary faculty members acknowledged that raising student achievement was unlikely unless struggling students spent more time in small, homogeneous groups working on "the basics." The parallel block schedule would mean that for at least one-third of each day classrooms would have no more than twelve students per teacher (Daugherty, November 11, 1998, p. A1).

As a result of involving elementary teachers and administrators in planning the new school, a truly innovative educational program had emerged. DeBolt was pleased with the result. The educators insisted, however, that one aspect of their former school be retained. Manassas Park Elementary School had pioneered a wonderful program to encourage students to write. Called "Wee Deliver," the program was modeled on the postal service. School corridors were given street names, and every classroom had an address. The United States Postmaster General even issued the school its own zip code. A third grade boy and girl were chosen to be the school's postmaster and postmistress. They helped coordinate the delivery of mail by younger students. Letters were written from students to other students as well as teachers. Parents sent letters to their children by way of the "Wee Deliver" system. Teachers sent mail congratulating students on their accomplishments. The unique postal system had helped create a sense of community at Manassas Park Elementary School, and none of the staff wanted to lose it.

Building on the "Wee Deliver" program, planners envisioned the new school as a small town. Each house would be a "neighborhood." The principal would become the "mayor." The hope was to design an environment that provided every student with a sense of "home," even as they moved from one class to another. DeBolt could not have been in greater agreement, since he long had maintained that schools, especially large ones, must attend to the "personalization" of education, a term inspired by *Breaking Ranks*, an influential report from the National Association of Secondary School Principals that called for sweeping reforms in education.

VMDO architects, led by Ken Thacker, took the ideas generated during the 1998 planning sessions and fashioned a design that reinforced the concept of an accessible and inviting community for young children. Scale was important. Though the school rose three stories, the entrance was only one story high, more in line with the size of the students. Everyone passing through the main entrance would pass the administrative offices, which were not hidden behind walls, but placed behind storefront-style plate glass windows. Office staff could wave to students as they arrived each day and also supervise who entered and left the building during other times. Bill Bradley noted that two design principles that had been followed in the high school also would be adopted for the elementary school. The principles were "visual openness and auditory privacy." Whenever possible walls contained lots of glass so students could see what was going on in *their* school. Even the room containing heating and ventilation equipment and other mechanical systems was given a "storefront" to allow students to see how the building operated. Noise, on the other hand, was minimized in public spaces in order to maintain an environment conducive to learning.

With an innovative design in hand and buy-in from elementary teachers and administrators, DeBolt faced 1999 with characteristic optimism that Manassas Park's financial situation would brighten and clear the way for construction to begin. He got his wish. The city, blessed with new revenues from residential and commercial growth, actually ran a surplus and, as indicated earlier, received the good news that its credit rating had been raised. By January 2000, work on the new school was well under way and, thanks to an unusually mild winter, ahead of schedule (Doherty, January 20, 2000, p. A3). Even more important, the project was within budget. The residents of Manassas Park, in fact, got a bargain in their new elementary school. The building costs amounted to only $80.30 per square foot, the second least expensive elementary school project of the fourteen schools placed under contract in Virginia in 2000. The statewide average cost was $92.99 per square foot.

DeBolt invited the community to suggest names for the new school. The old facility, Manassas Park Elementary School, would retain its name after it was renovated. Renovation, scheduled for January to August 2001, involved asbestos removal, new flooring, improved lighting, and replacements for cracked blackboards. Following renovation, Manassas Park Elementary School would house grades four and five, which had been located at Conner Elementary along with grade six, which would be relocated to the intermediate school, thereby transforming it to a middle school. Conner Elementary, which was in the worst condition of any Manassas Park facility, would be turned over to the city, probably to be demolished. Independence Elementary School, the home of the Early Childhood Special Education program and several kindergarten classes, also was slated to be closed.

In September 2000, school board chairman Frank Jones announced that the new school would be named Cougar Elementary School, after the mascot for the high school athletic teams. Rather than name the school after a local luminary, board members felt students would more easily identify with the mascot (Killen, September 21, 2000, p.A3). DeBolt notified the community that Cougar Elementary would be ready for occupancy by late January 2001, none too soon given Manassas Park's growing population. The enrollment for the entire district stood at 2,051, roughly double what it had been a decade earlier.

In order to effect the midyear transition from Manassas Park Elementary to Cougar, DeBolt orchestrated a highly participatory move reminiscent of the opening of the new high school. During the last weekend in January, teachers, local volunteers, and VMDO employees packed up instructional materials at Manassas Park Elementary. School buses were used to ferry boxes and furniture across town. DeBolt reckoned that the move fostered community building and cost savings at the same time, clearly a win-win situation for Manassas Park and its schools.

On January 30, 2001, students arrived at the new school and found their way to one of three separate, but connected, houses, each color-coded and designed to accommodate three hundred students in kindergarten through third grade. Each three-story house was referred to as a "city," and each city was designated by a different upbeat appellation—Sunshine, Evergreen, and Skyland. The three houses each contained twelve regular classrooms, one reading classroom, one specialist classroom, one science lab for twenty-five students, one social studies lab for twenty-five students, one technology lab for fifty-two students, three special education classrooms, one instructional leader office, and one counselor office. As planned, hallways in the 121,000 square foot facility were given street names. Kindergarten and first grade classrooms, for ease of access, were located on the first floor of each house. Second and third grade classrooms were located on the third floor of each house. In between, on the second floor, were located technology labs, music and art rooms, and science and social studies centers. Art and music teachers were especially pleased with the move, since they no longer had to be itinerant. Because DeBolt felt strongly that teachers were professionals and should be treated as such, all teachers had office space apart from their classrooms. Office areas in each house included computer stations for each teacher, general work space, and the amenities of a small kitchen.

Another special feature of Cougar was the media center. Designed roughly in the shape of a barbell, the media center contained an area where students could read quietly and do research and another area where teachers could read a story to a group. Connecting the two areas was a central desk and administrative area from which a librarian could supervise both locations.

True to its commitment to design a child-friendly environment, VMDO architects made sure that the scale of the building fit its young inhabitants. Everything from the counters in the main office to the windows along the stairways was child-sized. To make it easier for students to find their way, the color scheme for each house was used throughout the facility. Six hundred computers, all wired to the Internet, were available to help usher Cougar's students into the twenty-first century. Besides three fifty-two–computer academic "laboratories," Cougar was equipped with nine hundred computer ports, destination presentation systems with thirty-two-inch monitors, and video projection in each classroom and laboratory. Each regular classroom had four computers, and each social studies and science lab featured eight computers. DeBolt boasted to the local newspaper that Cougar Elementary, as far as he knew, had "more technological power than any elementary school in the world" (Schwab, November 16, 2000, p. A1). No one could accuse Manassas Park's superintendent of having modest plans for his school system.

Indicative of Cougar's "technological power" were the four monitors in the main hallway, each featuring live video from classrooms and other areas of the school. DeBolt wanted visitors to see the variety of activities going on at Cougar without disturbing teachers and students. Every student and every teacher had access to e-mail as well as the venerable "Wee Deliver" postal service. The "Wee Deliver" post office enjoyed a prominent location in the heart of the new school, a far cry from its exile in a modular unit at the old elementary school. Another pleasant change was the absence of modular units at Cougar. Manassas Park Elementary had tried to keep up with growth by adding twelve "learning cottages," as the unattractive modular units were dubbed. A fulltime network engineer was hired to keep all of Cougar's technology running smoothly. To reduce glare on computer screens, VMDO designed the school with ample indirect lighting.

Visitors to the new elementary school had to agree that it was a facility worthy of the most affluent school system. DeBolt had gotten almost everything for which he had hoped, and since his hopes were admittedly grandiose, he probably got more than he expected. Funds could not be found, however, to build a fourth "house" for the prekindergarten program. In order to provide space for special teaching centers, concessions also had to be made with the indoor physical education area. Instead of a regular elementary gymnasium with basketball goals, Cougar got a downsized fitness area that adjoined the multipurpose cafeteria. When the wall separating the two areas was removed, the room could be used as a small auditorium. Cougar almost wound up without a food service kitchen, but the wife of a school board member happened to be the cafeteria manager. When she objected to the shortsighted cost-saving measure, the kitchen was reinstated.

Recognition for Manassas Park's newest school was not long in coming. Not only did Cougar win accolades from students, parents, and teachers, but the Virginia School Board Association recognized VMDO with an award for the school's design (Cannon, January 9, 2002, p.A3). In his typically modest way, Bob Moje credited the process of stakeholder participation in planning Cougar for the school's recognition.

WHAT ABOUT LEARNING?

A wonderful new elementary school had been raised, but a crucial question remained to be answered. Could student achievement be raised commensurate with the quality of the facility? Improvements in learning had followed close on the heels of the new high school's completion. The process, however, would be somewhat more challenging at Cougar.

Ritchie Carroll, Cougar's first principal, previously was principal of Manassas Park Elementary School and Independence Elementary School. Having worked closely with most of the Cougar faculty before they moved across town to Cougar, she understood what they would be up against in the new school. Teachers felt that many children came from families that were not supportive of the school's mission. First grade teachers complained that students arrived in the late summer without the necessary prerequisites and reading readiness skills. The problem only grew worse in second and third grades. Teachers had just begun to use student achievement data as a basis for planning and instructional intervention. Some teachers harbored the belief that children from poor homes were less likely to succeed in school. Teachers' concerns and expectations clearly were mirrored in student achievement. When the third graders in 1998 took Virginia's initial Standards of Learning tests in language arts, mathematics, social studies, and science, the pass rates were 43 percent, 50 percent, 39 percent, and 54 percent respectively (*School Renewal Summary Report*, 2003, p. 7). On the Stanford 9 tests for second and third graders in 1998, Manassas Park Elementary School students fared little better, scoring below the fiftieth percentile in reading, mathematics, and science (*School Renewal Summary Report*, 2003, p. 7).

Manassas Park Elementary School's last years as a facility for kindergarten through third grade saw no substantial improvements in student achievement. Nor did the move to Cougar produce the hoped for "bounce" in test scores. Despite the surfeit of technology, the special centers, and the new organizational structure, Cougar found itself in the summer of 2002 in the unenviable position of being the only school in Manassas Park without state accreditation.

DeBolt normally began the new school year with a system-wide convocation in which he addressed all teachers and staff members. For the opening of the 2002–2003 school year, however, he chose to cancel the convocation and visit each school separately. The sole reason for his decision was to allow him to speak frankly with the Cougar faculty. DeBolt told them that they had let down the school system and its students. He reminded them of all the resources the school system had invested in Cougar. "I can't keep building new schools if we can't show any correlation between facilities and student achievement," he told the stunned audience. To this day there are Cougar teachers who still harbor resentment toward DeBolt for his remarks.

Whether it was his confrontational visit, the cumulative impact of improvement efforts, or simply becoming adjusted to the new school that made the difference is impossible to determine, but one thing is certain. Student achievement for the 2002–2003 school year climbed dramatically at Cougar. The pass rates in the four core areas all rose well above 80 percent, and the school achieved full state accreditation.

Aware that the early elementary program needed attention, Ritchie Carroll and her staff had launched a school improvement process six years earlier in 1997. Carroll had just been appointed principal of both Manassas Park Elementary School and Independence Elementary School, in the process becoming Manassas Park's first African American administrator.

In preparation for a formal site visit by a peer review team from the Southern Association of Colleges and Schools (SACS), Carroll organized a "School Renewal" process. Many of the issues that worried Carroll and her faculty were addressed in the course of developing a long-term school improvement initiative and planning the new elementary school. Carroll was especially impressed with the process used to plan Cougar:

> We had an opportunity to sit down around the table and discuss how we think student learning should take place with experts. What should happen? How should it occur? And then we were asked, What are your beliefs about the learning environment? The culture? What do you believe you would need in order to enhance teacher professionalism? Where do we need to be in the twenty-first century? And what would a school building look like?

Upon reflection, Carroll felt that participating in the planning of Cougar was one of the highlights of her career as an educator.

Once the move to Cougar had been accomplished, Carroll and her staff focused on implementing formative assessment processes that would yield the kind of data on student progress that could be used to identify areas of deficiency and plan remedial instruction. Dr. Gail Pope, the assistant superintendent, began to play an active role at this point, determining that Cougar would implement the Scott Foresman reading program and quarterly benchmark tests aligned to the Virginia Standards of Learning. Pope wanted teachers to make regular use of basal readers and reduce their reliance on guided reading texts. She also determined that a highly scripted reading program was not necessary as long as teachers understood how to use the Scott Foresman materials. To ensure that Cougar teachers received the assistance and training they needed, a reading specialist for the entire school system was hired. Virginia Bowerman, the reading specialist, initially was placed at Cougar and charged with ensuring that teachers taught from their literature-based basal readers. Bowerman helped teachers analyze their quarterly benchmark tests, spot areas where students were struggling, and provide timely assistance.

The school improvement process that Carroll launched was inherited by Dr. Pat Miller in August 2003 when DeBolt tapped Carroll to assume responsibility for human resources, transportation, food services, and building maintenance. Miller, who had served as principal of Conner Elementary and later as principal of Manassas Park Elementary (after Cougar opened), continued the focus on raising student achievement and simultaneously began to fine tune aspects of Cougar's operations and management. Among her goals were enacting the faculty's vision for Cougar, clearly defining performance expectations for students, and seeing that teachers participated in the continuous monitoring of student progress.

The vision that the faculty had adopted for Cougar read as follows:

Our vision at Cougar Elementary School is to prepare students to become lifelong learners and productive citizens.

The vision statement was reinforced by a school motto, mission statement, and list of shared beliefs:

Motto:

Believe, Achieve, Succeed

Mission:

Our mission is to promote academic success and lifelong learning by maintaining high expectations in a safe and nurturing environment.

Shared Beliefs:

All students are valued as individuals with unique intellectual, physical, social and emotional needs.

All stakeholders work collaboratively to provide and engage students with instruction promoting higher level thinking skills.

All staff members communicate high expectations for academic and behavioral performance.

The espoused mission may have addressed the need to promote academic success and lifelong learning, but no one on the staff of Cougar had any doubts about the actual mission—sustained academic success.

DeBolt had made it crystal clear that he had no intention of allowing one of Manassas Park's schools to fall behind. After Cougar achieved full state accreditation, it needed to press ahead to develop a truly outstanding program. Toward this end, a variety of changes were launched before Carroll turned over the reins to Miller. The "taught curriculum" was brought into line with the "tested curriculum." Pacing guides were adopted to help teachers cover all the necessary content before students took the state tests in the spring. Miller picked up where Carroll left off and made certain that the faculty met on a regular basis in vertical teams (all K–3 teachers in a house), grade level teams, and as a whole faculty to address concerns, maintain aligned curriculums, discuss struggling students, and monitor progress on school improvement goals. Teachers were trained in and became adept at disaggregating and analyzing student achievement data from benchmark tests administered during the year in preparation for state testing. Miller reduced the size of the leadership team to ensure that it functioned efficiently. Her new team consisted of a representative from each house (vertical team), the media specialist, and an ESL teacher. Meeting in the afternoon, the team engaged in troubleshooting and planning as well as discussing routine matters.

Miller continued the use of block scheduling at Cougar, thereby enabling teachers to introduce new content in heterogeneous classes while addressing specific academic concerns in small, homogenous instructional groups. Students in need of extra help had access to remedial software and the Saturday Institute. Miller and her leadership team took a hard look at after-school programs and summer school in order to clarify their purposes. They agreed that the primary objective of these efforts was to assist students who needed to pass the state tests, not to provide enrichment experiences.

The intensive focus on raising achievement required a heavy investment of time and energy on the part of the Cougar staff. To make certain that staff members felt appreciated and avoided burnout, Miller attended to a variety of school climate issues, including various forms of teacher recognition and opportunities for professional development.

If the faculty of Cougar Elementary School needed confirmation that their school improvement efforts were paying dividends, they received it soon after Miller became principal when a peer review team from the Southern Association of Colleges and Schools visited the school in the fall of 2003 and filed its report (Report of the Peer Review Team for Cougar Elementary School, October 13–14, 2003). The three-person team was charged with assessing the adequacy of Cougar's five-year "School Renewal" initiative, identifying strengths and areas in need of continued effort, and determining the extent to which the school complied with the SACS Standards of the Commission on Elementary and Middle Schools. The peer review team's report began by noting Cougar's "outstanding leadership" and the high level of staff involvement in the school improvement process. It went on to commend Cougar for achieving full accreditation status by the State of Virginia, based on the results of the 2003 Standards of Learning tests. Third graders jumped from 43 percent passing in English (reading and writing) in 1998 to 87 percent passing; from 50 percent passing in mathematics to 89 percent; from 39 percent passing in social studies to 84 percent; and from 54 percent passing in science to 86 percent. Substantial gains also were recorded for the Stanford 9 tests and the Phonological Awareness Literacy Screening (PALS) test. The report went on to praise Cougar for the high level of staff morale and the substantial amount of collaboration among teachers.

The "summary statement" of the peer review team's report provided clear evidence that Manassas Park no longer had anything about which to be ashamed when it came to the education of its youngest students:

> The Peer Review Team found Cougar Elementary to be an excellent school with a dedicated staff who holds the educational welfare of all students as the top priority in improvement efforts. The school provides a safe, clean, nourishing learning environment where the children, faculty, and staff are happy, well adjusted, and proud to be part of the Cougar family. A supportive group of parents and community members, volunteering their time and talents to assist and support the school, is reflective of a community that cares about the quality of education; these stakeholders take pride in Cougar Elementary's achievements. (Report of the Peer Review Team for Cougar Elementary School, October 13–14, 2003)

Three years after the peer review team's glowing report, Cougar was nominated for a National School Change Award. One of the supporting letters captured some of the school's special features.

To meet the needs of its population, teachers at Cougar instruct students in reading and mathematics in small groups of 12 or less. Instruction is diagnostically focused; teachers are well-trained in research-based strategies. Science and social studies specialists with exceptional content knowledge and pedagogical skills work with students in specially designed classrooms. Students also visit one of three technology centers daily for computer-based practice, reinforcement and enrichment of curriculum needs. Significant time is devoted to physical education and the arts as well. (Rettig, February 4, 2006)

Much of the credit for Cougar's success has to go to Ritchie Carroll, Pat Miller, and their faculty. At the same time, the role of central office leadership in school improvement should not be overlooked. In the next chapter some of the key contributions of the central office will be examined.

Chapter 5

A Foundation for Sustained Success

Much of Tom DeBolt's time during his first years as superintendent was spent in the community laying the groundwork for the school system's transformation. He had forged a very productive personal and professional alliance with Frank Jones, the school board chairman. Together they developed a relatively cohesive and supportive school board. Since school board members were appointed by the city council, this also meant cultivating close working relations with Manassas Park's governing body. DeBolt and Jones, as noted previously, became active in the local Republican Party for the express purpose of ensuring the nomination and election of council members who backed public education.

A supportive political environment is not the only ingredient, however, in turning around a troubled, low-performing school system and, just as importantly, sustaining the turnaround over time. It is one thing to garner support for building a new school or raising test scores and quite another to make certain that year in and year out a school system maintains first-class facilities and high levels of student achievement. Plenty of school systems have experienced a momentary spike in performance, only to settle back into mediocrity or worse.

Soon after taking the helm and assessing Manassas Park's circumstances, DeBolt recognized that his vision for a world-class school system was unlikely to move beyond the drawing board without attending to several concerns within the school system itself. Of particular importance to DeBolt were (1) the lack of a highly qualified and cohesive leadership team that shared his vision, (2) the absence of a systematic long-range plan to guide team members in their efforts to achieve the vision, and (3) the lack of a reasonable revenue-sharing agreement with the city of Manassas Park that would guarantee the resources needed to realize the vision. He believed that a capable leadership team, comprehensive long-range plan, and revenue-sharing agreement constituted an insurance policy against the predictable ups and downs of public education—demographic shifts, fluctuations in the economy, leader turnover, and the like. This chapter examines what DeBolt and his colleagues did to address this trio of concerns.

IT TAKES MORE THAN A LEADER TO MAKE A LEADERSHIP TEAM

Low-achieving school systems have trouble attracting talent. When they do manage to hire highly qualified individuals, they find it difficult to keep them. The first two decades of Manassas Park City Schools witnessed high rates of personnel turnover, especially among the ranks of school and division administrators. DeBolt understood that it is virtually impossible to maintain the consistency necessary for sustained improvement when leaders change every few years. He had made a personal commitment to stay the course, and he needed principals and central office administrators willing to make the same commitment.

Soon after his arrival in Manassas Park, DeBolt asked Arthur Gosling, a friend and fellow superintendent, to meet individually with Manassas Park administrators and give him feedback on their strengths and weaknesses. Gosling was brutally frank. He doubted that some individuals were up to the challenges of turning around a school system. Several lacked the passion for the job. Another person worried too much about undertaking any new initiative for fear of being sued. Others lacked the potential to significantly improve teaching and learning. DeBolt realized that he would have to rebuild his leadership team.

In the early years of his tenure, before salaries were raised to competitive levels and facilities were improved, DeBolt had to rely on a lot of cajoling and convincing to secure the kind of educational leaders he needed. There was little for newcomers to go on except DeBolt's rhetorical skills and his assurances that those who joined him eventually would be taken care of. Anyone can sell a Bordeaux from an established vineyard, but it takes a true salesman to interest someone in buying a new vintage from a fledgling winery. Tom DeBolt was a true salesman.

One of DeBolt's first hires was Ritchie Carroll, an energetic educator with extensive experience in early childhood and elementary education. After seven years of teaching in her native North Carolina, Carroll had moved to Manassas City and developed a program for at-risk four year olds. Dave Melton, DeBolt's assistant superintendent, got to know Carroll when she worked with his son, and he encouraged her to go into school administration. When the principalship at Manassas Park Elementary School opened up, he suggested that she apply. Carroll remembers her interview with DeBolt in the spring of 1996. Her initial nervousness disappeared when she realized that her interviewer already had done extensive checking on her background and capabilities and found her to be a good match for Manassas Park. Not only had DeBolt talked to her superintendent, but he had made inquiries with teachers and office staff. Hiring a principal was too important a decision, DeBolt believed, to rely solely on the standard written references.

Looking back on her move from Manassas City to Manassas Park, Carroll acknowledges that DeBolt's vision and style made the difference. Why else, she asks, would she have left a high-achieving school system with good facilities and high salaries? Then there was the fact that Carroll was African American, the first hired as an administrator in Manassas Park and one of only a few African Americans hired in any capacity during the school system's first two decades. Manassas Park, in fact, had a reputation for being inhospitable to African Americans. Her friends queried her. Why did she seek a position in a school system where she would be the sole person of color among two hundred employees? That she would consider such a move, however, indicated to DeBolt that she was just the kind of person he needed on his leadership team. Carroll had courage as well as commitment, and she would need both to assume the principalship at Manassas Park Elementary School. The staff was polarized and defensive. To add to her challenges, Carroll also was asked to serve as the principal of Independence Elementary School, the site of the special education preschool and kindergarten. DeBolt judiciously waited until after Carroll had accepted the principalship of Manassas Park Elementary to make the additional request. When she asked him why the dual assignment, Carroll was told that she had the experience to run an early childhood education program and, besides, the school system could not afford to hire another principal!

In 1999 DeBolt hired Pat Miller to be principal of Conner Elementary School, which housed the fourth and fifth grades at the time. Miller had taught in the Netherlands and served for eight years as assistant principal at the Islamic Saudi Academy in the suburbs of Washington, D.C. Why would a talented and highly experienced educator want to assume the principalship of a school in deplorable condition at a salary below that offered by neighboring school systems? Miller's answer was similar to Carroll's. She believed in what DeBolt wanted to accomplish in Manassas Park. Some educators seek the comfort of a school where students already are succeeding. Others welcome the challenge of lifting up a low-achieving school. Miller belonged in the second group, and it was this type of educational leader that DeBolt wanted on his team. The young people of Manassas Park did not need any more defeatists and managers with low expectations.

A second reason why Miller wanted to work at Conner was DeBolt's support for the use of a parallel block schedule at the elementary level. Miller was convinced that this type of schedule, coupled with some degree of teacher specialization, was just what was needed to raise student achievement. The traditional self-contained elementary classroom, she felt, was not adequate to the needs of many young students. With a parallel block schedule, she could provide additional instruction in reading and mathematics for students who needed it while allowing other students to pursue new academic challenges. To work well, the parallel block schedule required a high degree of teacher cooperation and shared responsibility. Miller knew this meant re-culturing Conner, but she was up to the task. By 2000, the impact of Miller's efforts began to be reflected in improvements on state tests.

With leadership at the elementary level in capable hands, DeBolt next turned his attention to the high school. Margaret Huckaby, the principal who had opened the new high school, resigned to accept a position in nearby Loudoun County. DeBolt began making phone calls to universities in the hopes of finding a promising recent graduate of an educational administration program. He knew that competition for high school principals was keen and that the pool of talented prospects was relatively shallow. Among the individuals who surfaced during DeBolt's search was a mild-mannered forty-four-year-old Nova Scotian who had come to the University of Virginia in the early nineties to earn a master's and a doctorate in education. Bruce McDade had taught secondary English for a number of years before coming to Virginia and, following his graduate work, served for six years as an assistant principal in a central Virginia high school.

DeBolt was impressed by McDade's academic orientation, his understanding of instructional leadership, and his extensive teaching experience. He knew that Manassas Park City Schools could not become a truly distinguished school system until its flagship facility—Manassas Park High School—gained a reputation for academic excellence. McDade grasped what was necessary for a high school to become a challenging learning environment. He also embodied high personal and professional standards, exemplified by his being chosen as the Doctoral Student of the Year when he graduated from the University of Virginia's Curry School of Education. McDade's dissertation addressed teacher perceptions of school leadership, a subject that would stand him in good stead as high school principal in Manassas Park.

When McDade accepted DeBolt's invitation to join the Manassas Park leadership team on July 1, 2001, he knew he could count on plenty of sage advice from his boss. DeBolt's first love was the high school principalship, and he had plenty of ideas about how high schools should be run. To his credit, however, DeBolt gave McDade room to put his own stamp on Manassas Park High School. At the same time, he freed McDade to focus on academic improvement and team building by minimizing his budgetary responsibilities. In a small school system, trust goes a long way. Instead of demanding extensive paperwork and elaborate justifications for cost items, for example, DeBolt trusted that McDade's requests were in the best interests of Manassas Park students. McDade, in turn, did not take advantage of that trust.

On July 1, 2001, DeBolt also welcomed a second addition to his leadership team. Gail Pope, the new associate superintendent for curriculum, instruction, and technology, boasted a lengthy resume that included work in the private sector, teaching experience, school administration, and a doctoral degree from Texas A&M University. After serving as administrative coordinator for instructional support services with Virginia Beach Public Schools and director of a regional Best Practice Center in Virginia, she agreed to join DeBolt in his quest to promote academic excellence in Manassas Park. Pope's portfolio might have intimidated someone with less extensive experience. Among her responsibilities were the following:

- Supervising the development, implementation, and evaluation of all K-12 curriculum and all state and federal grants supporting the curriculum

- Supervising the development, implementation, and evaluation of all special education and English as a Second Language programs

- Directing the activities of all technology personnel, ESL teachers, guidance counselors, and program directors

- Serving as the division director of testing and supervising the administration of all state tests

- Developing and administering all professional development programs

- Budgeting for and purchasing all textbooks and supplemental materials

- Overseeing the design, implementation, and evaluation of the division technology plan

- Serving as interim superintendent in the superintendent's absence

With Pope taking the lead on system-wide issues related to academic programs and professional development, Debolt could devote large portions of his time to mobilizing community support, working the local political system, ensuring the flow of adequate resources into the school system, and supervising capital improvement projects. Knowing that Pope could not exercise effective day-to-day oversight over all the programs under her jurisdiction, DeBolt obtained school board approval for the addition of a specialist in the most crucial area of the entire curriculum—reading. If Manassas Park was to become an excellent school system, DeBolt knew it had to ensure that all students could read at grade level or higher.

DeBolt's search for a reading specialist capable of supervising reading from kindergarten through high school resulted in the hiring of Virginia Bowerman in 2001. Finding a K-12 expert in reading was not easy, but DeBolt understood that adding a specialist who was only comfortable working with elementary teachers and students was insufficient. Despite the best efforts of elementary teachers, students with reading problems continued to enroll in middle and high school.

Expertise in reading remediation also must be available to secondary teachers. Bowerman had "the right stuff."

Bowerman started her career in education as a social studies teacher. After a stint in the private sector working for Xerox, she returned to education, earned a master's degree in reading, and landed a job as reading specialist in a private school. From that position, she moved to a public school system in Virginia and served as a middle school reading specialist. Bowerman was attracted to Manassas Park for several reasons. She liked the small size of the school system and the "positive feeling" that had begun to pervade it by the time she joined the leadership team. The people she met did not spend time complaining about why they could not raise student achievement. Instead, they expected that wonderful things could be accomplished through collaboration and hard work. She was prepared for both. Bowerman initially focused on working at Cougar Elementary with Manassas Park's youngest students. Later she moved her office to the high school where she could concentrate her expertise on reading at the high school and adjacent middle school.

As the years passed, DeBolt made other important additions to his corps of new leaders. He brought on board a new director of financial services, Jennifer Maguire; a new middle school principal, Elizabeth Purcell; a new principal for Manassas Park Elementary School, Eric Neff; and a new director of special programs, Mike Rolen. To ensure that members of the leadership team continued to grow, DeBolt encouraged them to attend conferences, pursue advanced degrees, and become active in professional associations. Knowing that his principals would benefit from a "sounding board" other than himself, DeBolt arranged for each one to have a mentor. Mentors included a retired principal and a university professor. They met periodically with each principal to discuss concerns and share new ideas. Not above being mentored himself, DeBolt arranged to meet periodically with a much-admired retired superintendent. He also was an active participant in the Virginia Association for Supervision and Curriculum Development, eventually serving as the organization's president.

DeBolt realized that an effective leadership team needed to be more than a "rubber stamp," a source of easy affirmation for his personal agenda. He expected the members of the team to offer open and honest feedback on his ideas and to provide guidance when conflicts arose. In 2003, the leadership team began to share responsibility with

DeBolt for planning summer retreats. Team members expressed a desire for opportunities to enjoy each other's company as well as reflect on the previous school year, plan for the coming year, and discuss new thinking about education and related topics. DeBolt secured school board support for holding the retreats in attractive locations.

During a spring planning session for the 2004 retreat, the principals decided that they needed to meet occasionally by themselves. Up to that time, they typically met only when the full leadership team convened. An insecure superintendent might have frowned on the idea of principals getting together on their own, but DeBolt actually was pleased that the principals, all of whom were relatively new to their positions, had begun to bond. Having been a principal, he also realized that there were certain issues best addressed by the principals alone.

One of the hallmarks of the leadership team retreats were discussions of thought-provoking books. Among the chosen books were Jim Collins's *Good to Great*, Malcolm Gladwell's *The Tipping Point*, Rhona Weinstein's *Reaching Higher*, and Michael LeGault's *Think*. Books were selected because they addressed aspects of Manassas Park City Schools' vision and strategic plan. The vision and strategic plan, in fact, were developed and fine-tuned during the summer retreats. The leadership team also used the summer retreats as an opportunity to involve the mentors in the collective reflection and planning process. As had been the case with VMDO architects, DeBolt believed in long-term relationships with outside consultants. In a very real sense, the mentors and even the architects were members of the "extended" leadership team.

Another hallmark of the summer retreats was the reporting of impressions regarding the state of the school system. One year, DeBolt shared what he had learned from a series of small group "conversations" with teachers. Another year, team members followed Bruce McDade's suggestion and interviewed employees in a unit other than their own. The objective was to find out what people across the school system, from bus drivers to coaches, thought was going well. The leadership team has been careful to balance attention to pressing problems with recognition of the good things going on in Manassas Park. Though they were all newcomers, leadership team members knew enough about Manassas Park's troubled history to appreciate the value of celebrating success. And there have been many such celebrations since Tom DeBolt became superintendent.

The leadership team also took on major responsibilities for recruiting and developing new staff members. Principals spent time in the spring traveling to college campuses and recruiting fairs in an effort to identify promising new teachers. By 2006 the principals were planning and coordinating the orientation program for new teachers as well as determining their schools' individual staff development needs. DeBolt felt strongly that his principals should function as instructional leaders, guiding teachers in the continuous improvement of teaching and learning.

CHARTING A COURSE TO SIGNIFICANCE

Prior to DeBolt's arrival, Manassas Park City Schools did not have a systematic plan for moving beyond mediocrity. In 1996, he pulled together five division goals, each with several specific objectives. Examined with the benefit of hindsight, the modest planning document seems more practical than visionary. DeBolt possessed an intuitive understanding that Manassas Park could not go from a struggling school system to a world-class operation in one giant leap. The five goals below, if achieved, certainly would not make Manassas Park excellent, but their accomplishment would position the school system to make a run at excellence.

Manassas Park City Schools
Division Goals

Technology	Appropriate instruction, technology, equipment and facilities will be provided for all students.
Student outcomes	All students will participate in educational programs designed to meet their present and future needs.
Staff development	A staff development plan will be implemented to assist each staff member to meet the goals of the school division.
Curriculum development	A comprehensive system for curriculum development, implementation and evaluation will be established.

Facilities   The construction of new facilities and
                                    the renovation and expansion of exist-
                                    ing facilities for every grade level in
                                    the school division. ("DIVISION
                                    GOALS," 1996)

By the summer of 2000, DeBolt could review these goals and feel some measure of satisfaction that progress was being made on each. With the assistance of several consultants, a comprehensive program of instructional technology was being implemented. Academic programs catering to the needs of high achievers, at-risk students, and non-college-bound students were either in place or on the drawing board. Staff development, especially related to instructional technology, was underway. The curriculum at all levels was being brought into alignment with the Virginia Standards of Learning. The new high school had opened to rave reviews, and Cougar Elementary School was under construction. Given these encouraging signs, DeBolt, the school board, and the leadership team could begin to aim higher

In the summer of 2000, DeBolt convened a three-day retreat in a rustic setting for his leadership team. This gathering would become an annual event, a chance for administrators to enjoy some leisure time together, explore new ideas, and assess progress. On the agenda for the inaugural retreat was a discussion of a long-range plan to guide Manassas Park City Schools into the twenty-first century. By the following summer, a six-year plan complete with vision and mission statements, goals, and objectives had been crafted. Incoming assistant superintendent Gail Pope was charged with overseeing and periodically updating the plan. The tone and contents of the plan were a far cry from the unassuming document that DeBolt had developed five years earlier. The introduction to the plan gave notice that new thinking was afoot in Manassas Park.

IMAGINE A FUTURE, CREATE A VISION

Imagine a district . . .
. . . where all educators, regardless of the positions, the subject they teach or their responsibilities, have at their fingertips
all the materials and resources they need; can locate student
performance information and possess the analytical tools to

use that information effectively; can get hands-on training instantaneously when needed; and can interact with a virtual community of professional colleagues.

Imagine a school . . .

. . . where every student, regardless of economic level, age, ethnicity, ability or disability, can select and use the resources needed for acquiring knowledge and becoming a good citizen; can reach out to the world and be immersed in the sights, sounds, and languages of other countries; and has opportunities to explore areas of interest and participate in a true community of learners.

Imagine a home [community] . . .

. . . where all parents, regardless of socioeconomic background or native language, can communicate readily with teachers about their children's progress; improve their parenting skills, and receive additional training, or even get a degree, without leaving home.

What is striking about these opening lines is their reach. Here is an invitation, not just to transform a school system, but an entire community. The mission statement that followed clearly indicated that the school system and the community needed to partner if educational excellence and accountability were to be achieved:

OUR MISSION: SUCCESS FOR EVERY STUDENT

In achieving our vision, Manassas Park City Schools makes a public commitment to the mission of:

1. Providing a positive learning environment, in partnership with parents, students, teachers and the community, that enables our students to become responsible learners, knowledgeable graduates, and involved citizens.

2. Achieving excellence in meeting the needs of each student, by being sensitive to individual differences, and by challenging each student to achieve his or her maximum potential.

3. Educating all our students to become lifelong learners, good citizens, and productive workers in a global society, able to utilize both traditional resources and the latest technologies to seek and use information, acquire and apply knowledge, communicate effectively, and solve problems for themselves and others.

4. *Providing a positive teaching-learning environment, which includes the careful measurement of learning and accountability by both students and teachers.*

When the six-year plan eventually was adopted, it contained six goals covering the areas of student outcomes, curriculum and instruction, school and community relations, technology, facilities, and personnel and compensation. These goals would guide the development of annual School Improvement Plans at each Manassas Park school and serve as the basis for resource allocation in the school system. The expectation was that the goals would stay the same over the six-year period, but that specific objectives under each goal might be "tweaked" in light of subsequent developments.

Student outcomes for the first time involved specific achievement targets linked to the state testing program. As the following achievement objectives indicate, DeBolt and the leadership team expected Manassas Park students to meet or exceed state requirements on standardized tests. In addition, targets for graduation rates and percentages of students enrolling in postsecondary education programs were set. To ensure that progress toward student achievement targets was closely monitored, the plan also required that achievement data be presented to Manassas Park educators and discussed. Data had to be disaggregated by student group in order to determine whether particular groups were demonstrating more progress than other groups.

ACHIEVEMENT OUTCOMES FOR SIX-YEAR PLAN

• By 2004, 75 percent of students in Grades 3–12 will perform at or above grade level in reading, language arts, and mathematics as measured by the Stanford 9 and achievement on SOL tests.

- All schools will reach full state accreditation by 2004 and maintain this level of accreditation thereafter. Full state accreditation is achieved when 75 percent of students in grades 3 and 5 pass the SOL tests in language arts and 70 percent of students in grades 3, 5, 8 and 9–12 pass all other SOL Tests.

- By 2007, the number of students completing graduation requirements will be 90 percent or higher, and the yearly dropout rate will decline from 3.3 percent to 2.5 percent.

- By 2007, as reported on senior surveys, 45 percent of graduating seniors will plan to enter four-year colleges, 40 percent will enter community colleges and technical schools; 5 percent will enter military service, and 10 percent will enter the work force.

- By Spring 2003, 75 percent of the students enrolled in the K-3 PALS Program will successfully obtain the end of the year benchmark score.

These objectives reveal much about the kind of leader DeBolt intended to be. He had no desire to set modest goals that could be easily achieved, thereby making him look good. If the school system could not perform on par with its more affluent neighbors, he would not be satisfied. His enormous expectations were reflected in the fact that the six-year-plan's original set of student outcome objectives went far beyond academic performance to include objectives related to student participation in extracurricular activities and student citizenship. DeBolt and the leadership team believed that school had to be more than classwork, homework, and test taking. Students, especially those from poor homes, needed exposure to a range of opportunities in order for them to identify special interests and cultivate gifts and talents. The ideal was a well-rounded student, one who was academically capable, but also someone who participated in a sport, club, or area of artistic expression and who exhibited good citizenship. Of eighteen student outcome objectives in the original plan, ten covered areas related to extracurricular activities and citizenship. While many educators, particularly adherents of the so-called "middle school philosophy," decried the negative consequences of competition, DeBolt and the leadership team embraced competition at all levels as a way to engage and energize students. The key was making certain that sufficient opportunities existed so that every student could find some endeavor in which to be reasonably competitive.

PARTICIPATION OUTCOMES

- By the end of the school year 2000–2001, each school will collect baseline data on participation; that is, each school will prepare a roster of activities and a tally of the number of students participating in each extracurricular activity at that school. (In the early years, these activities are often called "parent involvement." Therefore, elementary schools should examine these activities.)

- In the middle school and high school, student participation in extracurricular activities—in such opportunities as Debate Club, Beta Club or National Honor Society, "little" United Nations Club, art shows, band concerts and chorus performances, athletics, and drama, theatre, and dance presentations—will increase each successive year. By June 2002, at least 80 percent of the students in each school will be involved in two or more major activities each year. By June 2007, 90 percent of students in each school will be involved in two or more major activities.

- The middle school will implement an intramural program involving 30 percent of the students by 2001 and 50 percent of the students by 2003. An interscholastic sports program will be implemented in 2002–2003 and will involve 30 percent of the students by 2004.

- To maintain students' academic momentum, by 2003 the schools, working together, will develop and implement a transition plan to ensure successful upward movement from one school to the next in sequence. These transition plans will include curriculum alignment, buddy systems (student mentoring) between school levels, teacher and principal visits to the incoming classes, and class visits, with parents also in attendance, to the receiving school.

- During the 2001–2002 school year, the amount of family-centered activities will increase by 20 percent at the K-3 elementary school.

CITIZENSHIP OUTCOMES

- By 2007, evidence of responsible student behavior will increase by 25 percent, and evidence of irresponsible student behavior will decrease by 25 percent. **Additional funding for support positions in guidance, social work, counseling services and alternative education are needed at the middle school level. Additional options for placement of the highly disruptive students must be found.**

- By 2004, a service-learning program at the middle school and high school will involve at least 25 percent of the student body.

- The middle school and high school will initiate school spirit/ service groups to meet students' affiliation needs, as well as activity interests, for 100 percent of students.

- Attendance at all grade levels will increase from 93.5 percent to 94.5 percent by 2007; and attendance data will be disaggregated and reviewed and steps taken for improvement, if needed.

- Students at the K-3 elementary level will continue to participate in the annual St. Judes Children's Research Hospital Math-a-thon.

A number of these objectives eventually were deemed to be too specific for a broad planning document and consequently were dropped from the six-year plan. Manassas Park educators, however, continued to work on virtually every one of the participation and citizenship outcomes.

Competing academically with high-achieving school systems in northern Virginia, raising student participation rates in extracurricular activities to 90 percent, improving attendance, and lowering the incidence of student misconduct was a tall order, one requiring a variety of supporting goals and objectives. With regard to the curriculum and instruction goal, for example, the six-year plan called for expanded services for English as a Second Language students, consideration of an International Baccalaureate program for middle and high school students, increased enrollment in the prekindergarten program, and an extended school day for struggling students. Additional objectives included increasing the number of reading and math specialists at the secondary level, adding upper-level technology courses to the high school curriculum, implementing strategies to raise scores on the Scholastic Aptitude Tests, and doubling the number of Advanced Placement courses. To assist in the monitoring of student progress, one objective entailed the development and implementation of an online student records management system and another objective called for the development of quarterly online tests aligned to state curriculum standards. By administering these tests, Manassas Park educators could pinpoint areas where students needed help in order to pass the spring Standards of Learning tests.

Besides the core academic program, the arts received attention in the plan. Specific objectives dealt with the purchase of new band instruments and the collection and display of student artwork. Increased opportunities for students to engage in debates and dramatic productions were called for. The plan also entailed exposing Manassas Park students to performances by professional actors and musicians.

The third goal in the six-year plan focused on school and community relations and called for strengthening community support and improving student learning through parental involvement. The objective associated with this goal read as follows:

> By 2007, 80% of the parents of Manassas Park City Schools will indicate that they are informed in a timely and efficient manner about school activities and that opportunities for parental involvement are plentiful and appropriate.

Technology was the focus of the fourth goal, which entailed integrating technology into teaching and learning in all subject areas to enhance student learning and improve test performance. Technology to assist administrative and support staff in their duties also was noted. Specific objectives included developing an ongoing funding plan for replenishing hardware and software by 2002 and implementing technology to "deliver curriculum and enhance student learning" by 2005.

As might be expected, facilities constituted one of the six goals. When the six-year plan was drafted, only the new high school had been completed. Work was under way on Cougar Elementary, but Manassas Park Elementary School and Manassas Park Middle School still offered subpar learning environments. Two "big ticket" objectives, therefore, involved building new facilities to house the upper elementary and middle schools. Another objective called for the development of a system for electronically handling procedures related to building maintenance.

The ultimate success of most of the preceding goals depended on Manassas Park's ability to attract and retain a highly qualified professional staff. The sixth goal consequently addressed personnel issues, including compensation. The first objective involved achieving competitive salaries and benefits packages. School system officials were called on to "continuously compare salaries and benefits to remain competitive with the leading school divisions in Northern Virginia." Other objectives called for active recruiting efforts involving visits to colleges and job fairs, a special initiative aimed at hiring Spanish-speaking teachers, and an employee recognition program. One of the most ambitious objectives called for experienced teachers to teach classes with large numbers of at-risk students. Leadership team members felt strongly that the most challenging classes should not be assigned to the least experienced teachers. The neediest students deserved to be taught by professionals with proven track records.

Another major step in long-range planning was taken when the leadership team, school board members, and community members developed a six-year technology plan in 2003 and 2004 ("Technology Plan: 2003–2009"). It was not enough to have one of the six goals in the long-range plan deal with technology. Manassas Park intended to become a leader in the educational applications of technology. The lengthy and detailed document opened with the following mission statement:

> We are committed to preparing students for a world that is unknown to us in the present. Technological literacy makes students competent and confident. To ensure that students possess these qualities, the school division must ensure that technology is fully integrated into the teaching and learning process. It must also ensure that reliable information systems to support teaching and learning are in place and a professional development plan that supports ongoing instruction for all stakeholders is followed. The community recognizes the importance of technology in all aspects of the school division and supports the financial expenditures needed to keep technology working and to upgrade equipment as needed.

A review of Manassas Park's accomplishments in technology followed. Examining the list, it becomes clear just how important technology was in DeBolt's vision. Far ahead of most school systems of its size, MPCS boasted a well-developed infrastructure, widespread access to computers through labs and in-class hardware, a Wide Area Network engineer, a Local Area Network engineer, computer support technicians, online work order systems for computer maintenance and building repairs, and a computer-based telephone system supporting telephones in all classrooms. In 2004, the school system had more than 1,500 computers for an enrollment of 2,400 students.

The six-year technology plan included five general goals:

1. (Integration) Improve teaching and learning through the appropriate use of technology.

2. (Professional Development) Provide professional development and support programs that assist educators in helping students achieve high academic standards.

3. (Connectivity) Ensure that all schools have access to integrated instructional and administrative services across interoperable high-speed networks.

4. (Educational Applications) Promote the use of Web-based applications, services, and resources in all areas of the school division.

5. (Accountability) Assess all aspects of technology within the school division.

Consistent with DeBolt's belief that leadership is the springboard to improvement, the first "target" of the first goal called for administrators in MPCS to "have a vision and plan for technology use and integration." In order to facilitate the cultivation of a vision, extensive training for leadership team members was specified. Only after such training was professional development for teachers called for. DeBolt understood that it is difficult for administrators to monitor progress on a long-range technology plan if they themselves are not well versed in technology.

With the completion of the six-year plan and the technology plan, DeBolt had a roadmap to take Manassas Park City Schools from "good to great." This phrase and the book by Jim Collins for which it served as title had made a deep impression on DeBolt and the members of the leadership team. Their conversations frequently contained references to such Collinsisms as "getting the right people on the bus," "confronting the brutal facts," and finding the "hedgehog concept." After several years of working on the agenda in Collins's book, however, "great" would not be good enough for DeBolt. Believing that Manassas Park City Schools was capable of even more, he began talking about going from "success" to "significance." Early on he admitted that he lacked a clear understanding of what significance entailed in a school system, but uncertainty was no deterrent for DeBolt. He had faith that he and his leadership team together would figure it out. They took the first step in the direction of "significance" at their administrative retreat in the summer of 2004 when the decision was made to revise the school system's vision statement and craft a coherent set of organizational values.

Ritchie Carroll took the lead on pulling together various ideas to form a succinct and inspiring document, one that could be prominently displayed throughout the school system, a visible reminder of what Manassas Park City Schools stood for. Despite the pervasive emphasis on standardized test results, the leadership team agreed that a robust and motivating vision needed to focus on more than higher pass rates on state tests. The process of "re-visioning" was lengthy and eye-opening for Carroll. She had assumed that the members of the leadership team shared similar values and priorities. When it came down to agreeing on beliefs and a vision statement, however, the discussion sometimes grew heated. After reflecting on what the school system was expected to accomplish, its strengths and weaknesses, and the perspectives of various stakeholders, the leadership team finally began to close in on a set of guiding principles.

Following much wordsmithing, "To foster a learning community inspiring competence, confidence, and commitment" was chosen as the new vision statement for Manassas Park City Schools. The shared beliefs backing up this vision included the following:

- All things are possible.
- All children will learn.
- People make the difference.
- Empowered people make good decisions.

- Leadership embodies a mix of personal humility and professional will.

- Data drives decisions.

- Professional development is the cornerstone of our success.

Another component of the leadership team's re-visioning exercise involved articulating the school system's core values. Five values emerged from this process: people, commitment, community, quality, and clarity. In order to provide substance to these words, team members elaborated on each.

Under "people," they proclaimed the school system's dedication "to providing personalized attention to individual and group strengths and needs, honoring fairness, dignity, and respect." "Commitment" consisted of "persistently and passionately" pursuing the new vision for Manassas Park City Schools. "Working together as a family in the best interest of Manassas Park" constituted "community." "Quality" was described as meeting challenges with "creative and innovative solutions." The fifth value, "clarity," represented knowing where Manassas Park was headed and where it had been.

When the leadership team's work was complete, the vision, beliefs, and values were inscribed on wallet-sized cards and distributed to all school system employees. Wall hangings for the central office and every school and classroom were created. The vision statement and related items became a point of reference whenever the leadership team met and new initiatives were discussed. The last step in the process involved the development of a slogan that captured the essential character of the school system. The slogan, which was embossed on envelopes and letterhead, stated that Manassas Park City Schools is "motivated parents, community, & staff inspiring students." The authors of this slogan wanted to make it crystal clear that transforming an entire school system required a collaborative effort involving educators, parents, and community members.

THE FINAL INGREDIENT FOR SUCCESS

Manassas Park now possessed an inspiring vision, a comprehensive six-year plan, a technology plan, and a set of practical objectives for achieving the plan and realizing the vision. Only one piece of the puzzle was missing. DeBolt understood that all the impressive early gains could be in jeopardy unless the school system had continuing access to adequate resources. Having investigated funding practices in high-performing school systems, DeBolt knew that a key to stable funding involved a revenue-sharing agreement with the local governing body. Such agreements, however, were not easy to negotiate, especially in a fiscally conservative state such as Virginia.

One step toward a stable local funding formula for Manassas Park City Schools had been taken in the fall of 1998. The city's financial advisor, the same individual who had cautioned against building the new high school and elementary school, urged the school system to prepare a five-year budget plan (Bhagwandin, October 1, 2998, p. A3). The school board, under the leadership of Frank Jones, responded with an $80 million budget covering the period from 1999 to 2004. In addition to money for salaries, technology, transportation, and general operations, the budget included a substantial allocation for library books. DeBolt personally pressed for this item because the collection of print material in the school system was badly outdated. Jones was pleased with the five-year budget, but he also was a realist. When interviewed by a local reporter, he expressed the expectation that there would be considerable haggling with the city council before a final agreement could be reached.

Following the development of the five-year budget, the percentage of local revenues earmarked for the school system began to inch above 30 percent. DeBolt knew, however, that a significantly greater local contribution would be required if Manassas Park was to compete for talented educators with neighboring school systems and press ahead with ambitious improvement projects. At this point, DeBolt unexpectedly became the beneficiary of some timely advice from Chip Zullinger, his counterpart in Manassas City. Zullinger had commissioned an analysis of school funding in northern Virginia in order to see how his school system was faring. When he examined the report, Zullinger noticed that Manassas Park's figures for local support lagged well behind other school systems. DeBolt and the school board decided to use this information as a basis for forming a committee to investigate local funding and to commission their own comparative study. The committee consisted of two members of the city council, two members of the school board, the city manager and his financial advisor, and three citizens. Not one to leave anything so important to chance, DeBolt made certain that the three community representatives all had some expertise in financial matters. To provide school funding information for the committee, a consulting firm, Public Financial Management (PFM), was hired to prepare a report.

In the fall of 2003 the consulting firm presented its findings on local financial contributions to select school systems in northern Virginia (Summary of Local Financial Contributions to Select Northern Virginia School Districts, 2003). Drawing on Comprehensive Annual Financial Reports covering the period from July 1, 2000, to June 30, 2002, the report compared local contributions and related financial information for the cities of Alexandria, Fairfax, Falls Church, Manassas City, and Manassas Park and the counties of Arlington, Fairfax, Loudoun, and Prince William. The report also noted that, while the state of Virginia had developed a formula to guide its contribution to local school systems, many localities lacked a comparable arrangement to determine the amount of local revenue dedicated to public education. As a result, many school boards entered the annual budget development process with only a vague idea of what they could count on from local coffers. DeBolt and the Manassas Park School Board appreciated the point all too well.

The PFM report noted that a survey of fifty-six school systems in Virginia that had been completed in April 2000 found that nine school systems (16%) had negotiated revenue-sharing agreements with their local governing bodies. In January 2001, Manassas City was added to the list with an agreement that set aside on an annual basis 56.2 percent of the city's general nonagency revenues for the school system. The PFM report's authors identified the strengths and weaknesses of Manassas City's revenue sharing agreement ("Summary of Local Financial . . . ," p. 9):

> The revenue sharing agreement between the City of Manassas and its School Board has several strengths that benefit both parties. Some of these strengths stem from the benefits of any revenue sharing agreement, while some strengths are unique to Manassas.
>
> • The City of Manassas and its School Board can both benefit from substantive discussions rather than an annual debate over the dollar amount of money transferred.

- The revenue sharing agreement also allows for relatively accurate fiscal planning by the school district, which would be difficult without an agreement.

- In comparison to other districts, Manassas' revenue transfer sources are diversified. While some school districts rely solely on real estate and personal property taxes, the Manassas school district also pulls from several other revenue sources.

- MCPS are required to maintain a 15% reserve fund, which prudently hedges against potential funding shortfalls.

The general weaknesses of any revenue sharing agreement are applicable to the Manassas agreement, as well as other weaknesses that are particular to Manassas.

- The required 15% reserve fund may be viewed as a weakness in that the schools may wish to use this money directly on educational spending.

- The revenue sharing agreement under which Manassas operates does not include an adjustable funding floor, which is a weakness when compared to other revenue sharing agreements. If Manassas did have an adjustable floor, the schools would be assured that funding levels kept pace with inflation.

- The agreement includes a provision in which the City will use any excess General Fund revenues to bring the city's undesignated fund balance to 15% of the succeeding years' General Fund budget. This may create an incentive to underestimate budget projections as a precautionary measure.

- The predetermined transfer amount does not reflect population changes, educational policy changes, educational needs, the level of state aid, or the state index assignment.

- The revenue forecast information used to prepare the annual budgets is often not accurate enough to allow MCPS to maximize the use of its total operating budget.

As far as DeBolt and the Manassas Park School Board were concerned, the benefits of a revenue-sharing agreement clearly outweighed the disadvantages. The PFM report showed that only one northern Virginia school system—Alexandria—received a smaller share of local revenues than Manassas Park. In 2002, Alexandria schools got 29.7 percent of total general fund revenues as compared to 30.2 percent for Manassas Park schools. Fairfax County and Prince William schools, by comparison, received 46.9 and 47.00 percent, respectively. Manassas Park's city manager and financial advisor, however, were not particularly impressed. They prepared a presentation to the committee in which they attacked the PFM report and its figures. Fortunately for the school system, Michael Johnson, one of the three community representatives, knew enough about financial reports and statistical analysis to realize that the models and reasoning used to attack the PFM report were faulty. Placed on the defensive by Johnson's critique, the city manager and his financial advisor backed off and the report's findings were accepted, thereby paving the way for Manassas Park City School's first revenue-sharing agreement. None of the representatives on the committee wanted the children of Manassas Park to be shortchanged when it came to their education. The committee, in fact, originally sought an agreement in which the school system would receive on an annual basis 61 percent of local revenue. Given the city's other pressing needs, though, this figure was clearly unrealistic. DeBolt credits the hard work and persistence of Jennifer Maguire, his director of financial services and a key member of the leadership team, with the negotiation of a final figure of 57 percent. Manassas Park City Schools received a belated Christmas gift in January 2004 when the city council and the school board gave approval to the revenue-sharing agreement (Parrish, January 23, 2004, pp. A1–A2). Manassas Park's proportional contribution to public education suddenly vaulted over that of its neighbors.

DeBolt and the school board finally could breathe a sigh of relief, knowing that there no longer would be eleventh-hour negotiations to determine how much money the school system would receive. Veteran employees would not have to worry every spring about whether their jobs were safe. The revenue-sharing agreement gave DeBolt and the school board the financial support to press ahead with efforts to make Manassas Park salaries truly competitive. Without talented educators and classified staff, there could be no sustained transformation for the school system. No one could have been more pleased than DeBolt when he read the Virginia Education Association's 2005–2006 benchmark data for teacher salaries in Virginia (2005–2006 Salary Schedules for Teachers, November 2005). At the time he assumed the leadership of the beleaguered school system in 1995, starting salaries for Manassas Park teachers ranked forty-second out of 133 school systems in the state. By 2006, Manassas Park ranked fourth! At a starting salary of thirty-nine thousand dollars, new teachers in Manassas Park fared better than their colleagues next door in Manassas City (37,933). Only new teachers in Arlington (40,816), Fairfax (40,000), and Loudoun (39,600) received more. In terms of the maximum salary for teachers, Manassas Park ranked third at $75,117, behind Loudoun (77,705) and Manassas City (76,690).

Not only were Manassas Park teachers paid better than they had been in 1995, but there were more teachers on the payroll. The ratio of students to each teacher when DeBolt arrived was 14 to 1. A decade later the ratio had dropped to 12 to 1. Improvements were especially significant in the crucial early grades. For grades K-7, the student-teacher ratio fell from 17.7 to 1 to 13.0 to 1.

The building blocks finally were in place. Manassas Park City Schools had capable leadership at all levels, a detailed long-range plan complete with an inspiring vision, and ample resources. No longer were there acceptable excuses for providing anything less than a first-class education for the young people of Manassas Park.

Chapter 6

A Maturing Culture of High Achievement

The organizational history of Manassas Park City Schools to this point has been told largely in terms of critical incidents that helped to transform the school system. The hiring of Tom DeBolt. The forging of a political alliance between DeBolt and school board chairman Frank Jones. The completion of a grand new high school. Approval to build Cougar Elementary School. The development of a six-year strategic plan. The negotiation of a generous revenue-sharing agreement with the city council. Collectively these incidents contributed to the emergence of a new organizational culture, a culture no longer mired in resignation and mediocrity, but one characterized by professionalism, possibilities, and performance.

Organizational cultures are not developed overnight. Like landmasses forming around a coral reef, they emerge gradually. Once formed, a culture, by definition, is difficult to change. Tom Debolt discovered this fact when he took the helm of Manassas Park City Schools. By his account, it took almost a half-decade for people to begin to realize that their school system could accomplish great things. By 2003, evidence of improving student performance along with the completion of two new schools and other signs of success had begun to accumulate sufficiently to dispel any lingering doubts about what Manassas Park was capable of accomplishing. This chapter looks at the maturing of Manassas Park's culture of high achievement.

In the development of a new culture, which comes first, actual academic success or new beliefs about what students and educators are capable of accomplishing? In the case of Manassas Park, the process was iterative. Student achievement increased a bit. Beliefs changed a bit. Achievement rose some more. Beliefs followed suit. Along the way, there were a few setbacks. Cultural transformation of the kind experienced in Manassas Park is anything but linear.

The chapter opens with a review of Manassas Park's accomplishments, academic and otherwise. The second part of the chapter describes some of the more compelling characteristics of the new organizational culture of Manassas Park City Schools.

MULTIPLE INDICATIONS OF SUCCESS

In early August 2006, the Manassas Park City Schools leadership team met in Charlottesville, Virginia, for their annual retreat. Bruce McDade was promoted the month before to the position of assistant superintendent. Gail Pope, his predecessor, had left Manassas Park to assume the superintendency of neighboring Manassas City Public Schools. One of McDade's first responsibilities as assistant superintendent involved planning the retreat. He suggested that each team member share success stories from the school year just ended. The successes that were shared would have taxed the imagination of even the most optimistic Manassas Park educator ten years earlier. Few at the time could have anticipated the range and level of achievements.

Pat Miller and her two assistant principals, Pamela Terry and Stacey Mamon, opened the session with an overview of accomplishments at Cougar Elementary School. They began with an inspiring story of how the staff rallied to help one student overcome a variety of challenges and finally pass his third grade Standards of Learning tests. Next came comments about several new initiatives, including an innovative after-school reading program geared to the interests of young boys and a new partnership with Kaiser-Permanente. The giant health management organization agreed to "adopt" several poor families as well as donate school supplies. Miller proudly announced that more than four hundred parents had attended Cougar's inaugural Learning Luau, a gathering at which parents were apprised of the importance of the Virginia Standards of Learning tests. Miller also reported that three of her teachers were preparing to sit for the National Board of Professional Teaching Standards certification test. DeBolt agreed to pick up the expenses for the examination as well as supplement their salary if they obtained the prestigious credential. To broaden the expertise available to Cougar students, Miller announced that she had begun to hire teachers with dual endorsements in elementary and special education. The best news was saved for last. Cougar Elementary had just been named a Title I School of Distinction for 2006.

Eric Neff, principal of Manassas Park Elementary School, and Stephanie Cavedo, his assistant principal, spoke next. They opened by citing the band program. Every fifth grader had participated in the band program, the result of a unique new curriculum requirement inspired by Tom DeBolt. DeBolt felt strongly that many students from poor families never consider playing a musical instrument because they cannot afford to purchase an instrument or pay for private lessons. He secured school board support for purchasing two hundred musical instruments in order to provide one for every fifth grader. At the end of the 2004–2005 school year, rising fifth graders were invited to inspect a variety of instruments and choose the one they would most like to learn to play. Two retired band directors assisted in the process by evaluating students' physical characteristics and making recommendations. To accommodate the new fifth grade band program, long-time Manassas Park consultant Michael Rettig of James Madison University designed a modified parallel block schedule that preserved all the required time for instruction in core subjects while still providing significant time for music instruction. Students learned to play their preferred instrument during two fifty-minute periods on a six-day elective rotation. A zero period first thing in the morning and an after-school time slot were created to accommodate practice for the fifth grade bands.

Nothing less than a "world-class" music program for Manassas Park would satisfy DeBolt. He realized that such a program does not begin in high school. Like the best athletic programs, training must commence in the elementary grades. The first step was taken with the launching of the fifth grade band. The decision by 70 percent of rising sixth graders to continue with music in the middle school represented the second step. Once again the school board stepped up and supported the purchase of additional instruments.

Neff and Cavedo went on to describe advances on the remediation front. Manassas Park Elementary School got a reading specialist in 2005–2006 to work with small groups of students to correct specific reading deficiencies. Additional opportunities for academic assistance were created by shortening every period by five minutes. Doing so enabled Manassas Park Elementary School to offer a "zero period" when students in need of help could be given special attention while other students participated in enrichment activities. Another success story involved the expansion of after-school programs. Among the nine after-school offerings was "Girls and Guys Read," a new program designed to encourage pleasure reading. The program already had a waiting list.

The last item on Neff and Cavedo's list was a new mentoring program for beginning teachers. New teachers met monthly and set their own agenda. The intention was to address pressing issues early, before they led to frustration and instructional problems.

Liz Purcell and her assistant principal, Melissa Pitts, presented the successes for Manassas Park Middle School. They opened, as had the Cougar team, by describing how the staff had worked with several at-risk students to help them overcome problems and achieve impressive results. Of particular note was the improvement for special education students in the pass rate on the eighth grade state reading test from 8 percent to 42 percent. An extensive sports program for middle school students was implemented along with a variety of clubs, thereby giving students new options during and after school. Purcell went on to cite the continuing professional growth of the faculty and the addition of several talented new teachers. Most of the presentation, however, was devoted to detailing progress on the new middle school facility.

In the summer 2004, the city council approved a request from DeBolt and the school board to borrow 17.5 million dollars to fund a renovation and expansion project at Manassas Park Middle School (Parrish, August 17, 2004, p. A5). That the school system was able to undertake its fourth major building project in less than a decade was due in no small part to the productive political and personal alliance between DeBolt and Frank Jones.[1] Jones, the former school board chairman, had been elected mayor of Manassas Park in 2004. He proved an effective cheerleader for public education in his new role. Jones, who had originally become active in local politics because of his concern over poor school facilities, did not have to be convinced that the hastily constructed twenty-nine-year-old middle school needed substantial improvements. The collection of modular units that served as the middle school was sadly out of date and ill-suited to the school system's ambitious technology initiative. Since resources to level the old school completely and raise an entirely new facility were lacking, the plan called for renovating parts of the old facility, including the auditorium, and adding on new sections for classrooms and physical education. Construction and renovation would have to be undertaken while school was in session. Once again, VMDO architects were enlisted to come up with a "world-class" design.

Since space for expansion was limited, VMDO decided to add a second story. This was accomplished by building a new structure around the shell of the original facility. Classrooms were clustered in arrangements that facilitated the team teaching that had become a hallmark of the middle school under Purcell's leadership. The new school was outfitted for wireless reception, thereby eliminating the need for computer centers. Students had access to computers in every classroom. Day lighting was ubiquitous. Large glass panels in the cafeteria allowed middle school students to look across a wide expanse of lawn to their next academic destination—Manassas Park High School. DeBolt envisioned the lawn as a scaled down version of "the Lawn" on the Old Grounds of the University of Virginia. The new middle school contained several of DeBolt's "signature" features, including spacious and well-appointed workrooms for teachers. Workrooms had a desk and computer for each teacher plus a kitchen with a microwave oven, refrigerator, and dishwasher. DeBolt insisted on the dishwasher because he believed that teachers frequently got sick because they ate their lunch off unwashed dishes. As was the case at Cougar and Manassas Park High School, the middle school also was outfitted with plenty of mirrors so that students could check their appearance. All the mirrors once again were located in the hallways rather than the restrooms so that students would not linger too long with their preening.

DeBolt and VMDO were careful, as they had been with previous building projects, to solicit plenty of teacher input before developing a design for the middle school. If a school was to be a professional environment—and DeBolt insisted that it must be—teachers needed to have a hand in planning it. To further enhance teacher buy-in, DeBolt arranged for the middle school staff to tour the unfinished facility in March 2006, six months prior to the scheduled opening. When teachers arrived, they found their own hardhats had been provided, a symbolic gesture intended to reinforce the idea that the school was theirs.

Connecting the middle school and the high school was an impressive new athletic complex containing gymnasiums, locker rooms, offices for coaches and physical education teachers, and a wrestling facility. DeBolt was especially proud of this section of the new school. He boasted that the wrestling area rivaled similar space in any college. To make sure coaches and physical education teachers were treated as professionals, first-class offices with showers and private lockers were provided. DeBolt and VMDO recognized that seemingly minor details—showers in coaches' offices and kitchens in teachers' workrooms—meant a great deal to users.

When Purcell and Pitts had finished their update on the new middle school, it was time for the high school's success stories. Tracy Shaver, the new principal and former assistant principal under McDade, and Laura Cross, the recently hired assistant principal from Fairfax County, opened with the announcement that 93 percent of the high school students passed their state Standards of Learning tests and twenty-six students achieved perfect scores of six hundred. For the fifth year in a row, Manassas Park High School achieved full state accreditation. Furthermore, the school met Adequate Yearly Progress under the No Child Left Behind Act for the third year in a row. The combined average score on the Scholastic Aptitude Tests (verbal and quantitative) was 1010, the highest in the history of the high school and a substantial improvement over the previous year's 926 average. Advanced Placement examinations were taken by seventy-six students, up by fourteen students from the previous year.

So successful was Manassas Park High School at involving students in Advanced Placement and dual enrollment courses that Jay Mathews, education editor of the *Washington Post*, cited it as one of the top high schools in the nation. Opportunities for Manassas Park students to gain college credit while still in high school had been expanded when Manassas Park High School chose to participate in Governor Mark Warner's Early College Scholars program. The governor honored Manassas Park High School and thirty-nine of its peer institutions at a special reception in Richmond because of the high percentage of seniors who participated in the program. In 2004–2005, twenty-eight Manassas Park students, representing 30 percent of the senior class, completed the program. The high school also operated the Bridges program to make it possible for students to get a head start on community college work.

Of the 2006 graduating class of ninety-two students, 85 percent went on to some form of postsecondary education. Of this group, 51 percent entered a four-year college and 34 percent enrolled in a community college. For a school system once derided for low expectations, these statistics were very impressive.

Shaver and Cross did not stop with academic achievements. They expressed pride in the fact that 51 percent of the high school students participated in at least one sport or extracurricular activity. The new Multicultural Night event was well attended and featured performances by a large number of students representing different cultural backgrounds. With regard to the high school faculty, ten teachers had perfect attendance during 2005–2006 and thirty-six teachers posted three or fewer absences. One hundred percent of the high school faculty had developed their own Web site in order to enhance community outreach. The high school began to engage in "horizontal teaming" in order to break down disciplinary divisions. Under this arrangement, teachers who worked with students at a particular grade level met periodically to discuss issues on a student-by-student basis. Previously, teachers had tended to meet only by academic specialty. Another "success" was the scheduling of English 11 Honors on an everyday, as opposed to an alternating day, basis. By meeting daily, students in English 11 Honors could spend more time preparing for the Scholastic Aptitude Tests. A key objective of the high school was to continue to improve student performance on the Scholastic Aptitude Tests.

The reports from each school at the 2006 leadership team retreat provided convincing evidence of the healthy state of affairs in Manassas Park City Schools in 2006. Another way to appreciate the progress made during the first decade of Tom DeBolt's superintendency is to compare the percentages of students passing state Standards of Learning tests in 1998, the first year the tests were administered, and 2005. Table 6.1 contains pass rate data on reading and mathematics tests for third, fifth, and eighth grades. Table 6.2 contains pass rate data for high school end-of-course tests in English, writing, Algebra I, Geometry, and Algebra 2. Across-the-board double-digit gains offer dramatic proof of what can be accomplished when a school system and a community commit to a systematic program of improvement. What is even more impressive is to realize that these gains were achieved during a period when Manassas Park's Hispanic population climbed from 13.5 percent to 38.0 percent, when the percentage of students designated as Limited English

Table 6.1. Standards of Learning Test Pass Rates, Grades 3, 5, and 8, 1998 and 2005

	3rd Grade English	3rd Grade Math	5th Grade Reading	5th Grade Math	8th Grade Reading	8th Grade Math
1998	43.27	50.00	53.97	19.84	68.25	68.55
2005	83.14	91.16	86.55	85.71	80.41	82.74

Proficient (LEP) rose from eight to 24.9, and when the percentage of students eligible for free and reduced price lunch jumped from 29.0 to 35.1. ("Manassas Park City Schools: The Transformation of a School Division, 1994–2005," 2006). By 2006, each of the school system's four schools was fully accredited by the Virginia Department of Education and the Southern Association of Colleges and Schools. Manassas Park was one of only fifty-one school divisions out of Virginia's 133 that were fully accredited by the Southern Association of Colleges and Schools (School Board Minutes, May 16, 2005, p. 3). Each Manassas Park school also achieved Adequate Yearly Progress under the No Child Left Behind Act.

Manassas Park's successes were not limited to test scores and accreditation status. In athletic competition, Manassas Park teams distinguished themselves, in the process fostering great pride across the community. The wrestling team won a state championship, and the football team came within one point of doing so. The girls' softball team joined the wrestling and football teams in becoming perennial district favorites. Manassas Park musicians and debaters garnered awards. The high school's Fashion Show provided an opportunity for students to

Table 6.2. Standards of Learning End-of-Course Test Pass Rates, 1998 and 2005

	English Reading/Lit	Writing	Algebra 1	Geometry	Algebra 2
1998	68.18	63.83	21.62	72.22	30.77
2005	97.20	97.60	95.19	90.40	95.31

show off their designs and receive recognition. Even the facilities achieved notoriety. Manassas Park High School was chosen as an exemplar of learning-oriented school construction (Feller, 12-1-05, pp. 1, 3), and Cougar Elementary won high praise from architects and educators.

While many communities would have paid dearly to see their public schools attain such success, the residents of Manassas Park enjoyed educational excellence at bargain basement prices. For fiscal year 2006, for instance, the per pupil cost to educate a Manassas Park student was $10,766. This figure compared very favorably to most of the school system's neighbors. Per pupil costs in Fairfax County were $11,915, while Arlington spent $16,464 to educate each student. Of the $10,766 spent on each Manassas Park student, $6,255 came from local revenues, $817 from state sales tax, $3,176 from other state funds, and $518 from federal sources ("Manassas Park City Schools: The Transformation of a School Division, 1994–2006," 2006).

Additional evidence of the school system's frugality was provided at the February 22, 2005, meeting of the school board. DeBolt presented information on Manassas Park's energy management initiative (School Board Minutes, February 22, 2005, pp. 2–3). In the first nine months of the initiative, MPCS achieved a 35 percent cost avoidance, thereby saving the taxpayers of Manassas Park almost $213,000. This figure meant that the school system was in first place for energy savings, not only for school systems in Virginia, but for the entire mid-Atlantic region.

FEATURES OF MANASSAS PARK'S NEW ORGANIZATIONAL CULTURE

The accomplishments recorded by Manassas Park City Schools following Tom DeBolt's arrival in 1995 contributed to and were products of an emerging culture of high achievement. Each new report of student success on state tests, each athletic championship, each gleaming new facility served to inspire confidence and bolster the image of Manassas Park as a school system where success was more than a distant dream. This section examines some of the central elements of Manassas Park's new organizational culture.

Organization theorist Edgar Schein (1985, p. 9) defined organizational culture as "a pattern of basic assumptions—invented, discovered, or developed by a given group as it learns to cope with its problems of external adaptation and internal integration—that has worked well enough to be considered valid and, therefore, to be taught to new members as the correct way to perceive, think, and feel in relation to those problems." Schein contended that culture is formed as organizations grapple with the twin challenges of adapting to their environments and ensuring that members of the organization continue to pull in the same direction.

Not all organizational cultures, of course, are robust and productive. For the first two decades of its existence, Manassas Park City Schools was characterized by a culture of defeatism and low expectations. Educators assumed that they had to learn to live with whatever meager resources the city council chose to bestow. Few people expected the working-class families of Manassas Park to harbor high aspirations for their children. If parents truly desired a first-class education for their children, they had to move to Fairfax County or the City of Manassas. Expectations for Manassas Park educators were as modest as those for the children they taught. It was taken for granted that Manassas Park could not attract talented educators. If a few promising individuals happened to land in the school system, they certainly would not stay for long. Mismanagement and organizational dysfunction were grudgingly accepted as the lot of the renegade city.

One need only look at the belief statements adopted at the 2004 leadership team retreat to realize that Manassas Park's self-image was changing, and with it, the school system's organizational culture. "All things are possible. All children will learn. People make the difference. Empowered people make good decisions." And so on. These were not the shibboleths of people who contented themselves with mediocrity. The educational leaders who crafted these statements were believers in the power of teamwork and positive thinking. They had seen what could happen when educators insisted on high achievement.

An organization's culture often can be detected in the expressions that people use, and the expressions heard in Manassas Park frequently originated with Tom DeBolt. Mention already was made in the last chapter of DeBolt's devotion to the terminology in Jim Collins's *Good to Great*. An avid reader, DeBolt picked up terms such as "execution," "passion," and "client-centered" from contemporary books on executive leadership. Eventually these terms surfaced in conversations among leadership team members. When DeBolt spoke of Manassas Park's new facilities, he referred to them as "world-class." He also wanted the academic program, the music program, and the athletic program to be "world-class." The term *personalization* frequently was heard in discussions among Manassas Park educators. It connoted the expectation that students would be treated with care and respect and that their individual needs and aspirations would be taken into account.

Convinced that the school system had demonstrated that it could achieve "success," DeBolt began to press his leadership team to move toward "significance." That no one, including DeBolt, was especially clear about what "significance" entailed mattered little. He was confident in the power of "teamwork." A clear conception of "significance" eventually would emerge as long as people persisted and thought hard.

Organizational culture also is revealed in what people value. Manassas Park educators clearly valued the school system's small size. When the six-year plan was written, the drafters included the following statement:

> Manassas Park is proud to be small. Our students, parents, and teachers know each other. Everyone benefits from the warmth and openness and attention to individual needs made possible by the size of the district. In Manassas Park, no student is "just a number" and no school is an "education warehouse." ("Vision, Mission, Goals, and Objectives," p. 8)

Students were not alone in being beneficiaries of Manassas Park's small size. The voices of teachers and other staff members were highly valued. DeBolt and the architects from VMDO consulted school employees prior to designing each new facility. Teachers provided important input regarding classroom layout, scheduling, teacher work space, and other features of Manassas Park High School, Cougar Elementary School, and Manassas Park Middle School. Mention was made in the last chapter of DeBolt's conversations with staff members and the staff interviews conducted by leadership team members prior to the 2005 administrative retreat. In April 2006 Gail Pope conducted a "Summit for Success" with sixteen of Manassas Park's most outstanding teachers. They were asked to discuss the following question: What are the characteristics of a quality teacher both in the classroom and when fulfilling professional responsibilities beyond the classroom? Their responses were recorded, and then Pope asked them how this information should be used. The teachers suggested that their notions of a quality teacher should be shared with new teachers and used as the basis for interviewing prospective new hires. One novel suggestion was to videotape teachers demonstrating the elements of quality instruction and make the tapes available to teachers in need of assistance.

Community voices also were valued by school system leaders. Citizens provided advice on where to locate school facilities, the grading scale used in Manassas Park, school discipline, and many other matters. A particular effort was made to understand the concerns of Manassas Park's growing Hispanic population. The school system hired a Spanish-speaking community liaison to facilitate this process.

Mention already has been made of the value placed on educating well-rounded students. Manassas Park educators clearly believed that academic excellence was an important goal for young people, but they had no desire to graduate one-dimensional "eggheads" who lacked social skills, good manners, or an appreciation for the arts and physical fitness. To encourage "well-roundedness," Manassas Park developed a *balanced* program of academic and extracurricular programs that provided opportunities for all students to achieve recognition. The high school's lofty goal of getting 100 percent of its students involved in at least one sport, club, or performing art bespoke the school system's commitment.

Good character is an important component of a well-rounded student. Manassas Park participated in the national Character Counts program, which stressed the importance of "six pillars of character"— respect, trustworthiness, responsibility, fairness, caring, and citizenship (Parrish, October 26, 2004, p. A1). To cultivate good citizenship, students had opportunities to give back something to the community. Elementary students held fundraisers for various charities. High school students hosted senior citizens for a Valentine's Day social and collected money to help the victims of Hurricane Katrina.

When it came to the conduct of Manassas Park's professional staff, shared responsibility was the cardinal virtue. A key to the school system's academic improvement, in fact, was the emphasis placed on groups of teachers meeting, reviewing student progress, and developing provisions to assist struggling students. Virginia Bowerman boasted that Manassas Park educators refused to give up on any student, no matter how much they might be struggling.

Teamwork was built into the instructional programs of all four Manassas Park schools. Perhaps there was no better illustration of the ethic of shared responsibility, however, than the absence of assigned disciplinary duties at Manassas Park High School. Practically every high school in the United States annually assigns teachers to hall duty, cafeteria duty, locker room duty, parking lot patrols, and the like. Not so at Manassas Park High School. Because staff members bought into the value of shared responsibility, anyone who encountered inappropriate behavior intervened. Adults did not ignore misconduct just because someone else was expected to deal with it.

Another value that characterized Manassas Park's organizational culture concerned attention to detail, especially when it came to how things looked and how they functioned. The focus on appearances was not surprising, given the school system's history of shoddy facilities and second-best equipment and materials. Some folks might argue that effective education can occur anywhere. Manassas Park educators learned the hard way, however, that it mattered where students were schooled. Clean and attractive facilities were an invitation to take education seriously and a symbol of the high regard in which schools were held by local residents. DeBolt and his principals routinely inspected their facilities to see that anything in need of repair was handled expeditiously. The maintenance crew at each school took great pride in their work.

A seemingly minor matter—the condition of playing fields—illustrates DeBolt's obsession with quality. He delighted in telling people that he had a "dirty mind," by which he meant that he took the soil on which athletic events were staged very seriously. DeBolt was critical of some of the school systems against which Manassas Park competed because they settled for playing fields that were not level or well maintained. Such surfaces invited injury and reflected a carelessness that he implied could carry over to academics. DeBolt was known to take up much of an administrative meeting lecturing leadership team members on the best ways to fertilize the football field and baseball diamond. He described at length the difficulties of Virginia's red clay soil and insisted that Manassas Park groundskeepers use "magic sand" from Mississippi to break down the clay and encourage lush turf. While his waxing eloquent on the quality of soil and the proper way to fertilize were the subject of numerous good-natured jests, members of the leadership team knew that DeBolt's concerns were rooted in a reverence for doing things right. His beliefs proved to be highly contagious.

Another hallmark of an organization's culture is its routines and rituals (Deal & Kennedy, 1982). Recurring events often embody and symbolize the assumptions, beliefs, and values considered "sacred" by organization members. It was never too early to introduce newcomers to "the Manassas Park way." No sooner did new teachers arrive for orientation in August than DeBolt took them on a bus tour of Manassas Park. As the bus rumbled from neighborhood to neighborhood, DeBolt apprised his audience of the city's checkered history and how far it had come since 1975. The tour provided him with an opportunity to point out the modest residences in which many students lived and to underscore how much their hopes depended on what the school system could offer in the way of opportunities.

DeBolt was not alone in his penchant for routines. Come report card time, Bruce McDade could be found hand-delivering report cards to parents who, for some reason, failed to pick up their child's report card at the high school. Small gestures like this pervaded the school system and reinforced the notion that students and what they did in school were important.

The necessity of teamwork was stressed at the annual convocation of school system employees that opened each school year. DeBolt insisted that all employees attend, from classroom teachers to food service personnel. No excuses. The convocation served as a visible symbol of collaboration, the crucial element in Manassas Park's transformation. Everyone must feel a part of the process. The convocation typically involved an inspiring guest speaker, but as well it offered DeBolt an opportunity to laud people for their accomplishments and remind people of the school system's unfinished agenda.

Teamwork also was emphasized during "moving day" when a new facility was prepared for opening. School was suspended across the system, and teachers, parents, community members, and students joined in loading boxes, moving furniture, directing traffic, and unpacking. Such experiences reinforced the community spirit that had become an effective antidote to the negativism that prevailed in Manassas Park's past.

An important feature of Manassas Park's culture involved valuing and celebrating success. Few opportunities to recognize achievement were overlooked, whether it was student performance on state tests at

Cougar and Manassas Park Elementary, fundraising for charity at Manassas Park Middle School, or the 600 Club at Manassas Park High School. Athletic teams each had their Player of the Year, but just as important were the weekly Sportsmen of the Week who exemplified good character on and off the playing field. Manassas Park's Character Counts program recognized students who demonstrated the qualities associated with high personal standards of conduct. Each school also provided awards for students with excellent attendance.

One of Manassas Park's most enduring rituals was the "Expectations of Excellence" ceremony held at the high school several weeks after the beginning of each school year. Inaugurated soon after DeBolt took over as superintendent, the event honored students who had achieved academic distinction. Academic letter winners for the preceding school year were announced, National Honor Society members were recognized, and members of the 600 Club were introduced. The ceremony culminated with the announcement of the Most Valuable Cougar, the senior who best exemplified academic excellence. Bruce McDade characterized the ceremony as an "academic pep rally." By holding it as a kickoff event, Manassas Park educators set the desired tone for the coming year and inspired students to do their best. Other school systems tended to hold awards ceremonies at the end of the school year, thereby missing an opportunity to motivate students as they faced current academic challenges.

Other occasions during which success was celebrated included groundbreakings and graduations. Opening a new school was a major accomplishment for a relatively revenue-poor community such as Manassas Park. DeBolt and the school board staged groundbreakings so that local residents could receive thanks from the school system and participate symbolically in the process of improving the learning environment for local youngsters.

Perhaps no ritual captured the character of Manassas Park's culture of high achievement better than graduation from Manassas Park High School. Festivities began with Senior Day, an occasion for the high school administration to acknowledge the special qualities and contributions of each and every graduate. Senior Day was not a time for "the best and the brightest" to walk off with all the awards. Bruce McDade's wife, Norbi, spent the month leading up to Senior Day making a personalized doll for every graduate. The dolls were lined up on a table when the seniors arrived. Each doll had the student's hair color, sports insignias, academic tassle, and other distinguishing features. Presenting each student with his or her likeness symbolized the fact that they were known and valued as individuals.

Graduation followed Senior Day, and it was the high point of the school year in Manassas Park. On their way to the ceremony, each senior rang the "bell of knowledge," just as they had done on the day fours years earlier when they first arrived at the high school. In the audience at graduation were not just high school teachers, but elementary and middle school teachers as well. The school system recognized that it took the efforts of teachers from every level to ensure that a student earned a diploma. Those attending graduation always heard from the student salutatorian and valedictorian as well as an invited speaker, usually an individual who overcame great odds on the road to personal and professional success. Graduation, of course, would not be graduation without remarks from the superintendent. DeBolt never missed an opportunity to remind people how far the school system had come and how fortunate the students were to have such excellent teachers and facilities and such supportive parents and taxpayers. A good education, he asserted, was nothing to take for granted.

A recent addition to Manassas Park's collection of rituals was a ceremony of recognition for teachers who achieved continuing contract status (the equivalent of tenure). In most school systems across the United States, tenure means a form letter in a teacher's office mail box. The Manassas Park leadership team decided that the passage from probationary to permanent employment status should be regarded as an honor and a major accomplishment. Manassas Park teachers who crossed the professional threshold were recognized with a special plaque and an appearance before the school board.

In the long run, if Manassas Park is to sustain its impressive turnaround, it probably will be due in large part to the development of a robust organizational culture. Long-range plans and revenue-sharing agreements are vital, but they are no substitute for an enduring set of beliefs, values, and customs that remind people every day that success is possible and that it can be achieved without sacrificing caring and concern. Unlike many school systems, Manassas Park undertook the process of culture building in a very deliberate and focused way. Creating a constructive culture of high achievement was simply too important to leave to chance.

Chapter 7

A Future Full of Questions

The primary focus of this book are the years from 1995 to 2005—the first decade of Tom DeBolt's superintendency—and the impact of this transformative period on the Manassas Park City Schools. It is always difficult to bring to a close the history of a dynamic organization. The previous chapter, for example, trickled into the 2005–2006 school year. All organization histories, of course, must stop at some point, if only to permit reflection on what was accomplished, assessment of lessons learned, and prediction of future challenges. Chapter 7 addresses the third activity.

It is hard enough to deal with the past and the present with some degree of clarity. The future remains forever vague. Consequently, it seems appropriate to organize the present chapter around several questions that were keeping Manassas Park leaders awake at night as this book was being completed. Question number one concerned demographics. Many local observers sensed that the ethnic makeup of Manassas Park, like other cities across the country, was changing rapidly. If this shift continued, what would the school system need to do in order to accommodate the change?

Resources are a perennial question mark, even with a solid revenue-sharing agreement. It is difficult to sustain success without stable funding. DeBolt and the school board wondered what would happen if the housing market cooled or the flourishing local economy stalled.

A third question on the minds of many folks in Manassas Park concerned the political alliance between Tom DeBolt and the city council. Political alliances do not last forever. Could this one hold long enough to see DeBolt's dream of a school system with four world-class schools become a reality.

Then there was the issue of performance. It was one thing to ask local taxpayers to make sacrifices to support a high-performing school system, but what if Manassas Park's academic and extracurricular successes could not be maintained? No school system ever can afford to take student achievement for granted, especially in a highly competitive environment such as northern Virginia where parents keep a close eye on test scores in neighboring school divisions.

The last question concerned DeBolt himself. At some point he would retire or resign. What would Manassas Park City Schools do without him? Could any succession plan accommodate the loss of such an influential leader? Had the school system matured to a point where it could endure transition at the top without loss of momentum?

HOW WILL MANASSAS PARK COPE WITH CHANGING DEMOGRAPHICS?

Demographics are on the mind of most educational leaders, for obvious reasons. State funding for public schools is tied to student enrollment. Enrollment increases occasion the need for more teachers and support staff and, ultimately, expanded facilities. Shrinking enrollments necessitate the painful process of staff reduction and, eventually, school consolidation and closure. Leaders such as Tom DeBolt do not like to be surprised when it comes to demographic changes. They invest considerable time and resources in trying to anticipate enrollment trends. Not only do they seek to know how school enrollments are apt to change, but they also want to know the characteristics of students who will be moving into and leaving the school system. Such knowledge is critical for planning and budgeting.

Manassas Park sits in the midst of one of the nation's fastest growing areas (Cohn & Gardner, March 16, 2006). Many jurisdictions in northern Virginia are growing at an annual rate of 1.5 to 5.9 percent, but some areas, such as Loudoun County, Manassas Park's neighbor to the west, exceed 8 percent. Since Manassas Park is relatively small and almost completely built out, the prospects for substantial enrollment increases are somewhat limited. A significant jump in population would require converting commercial space and aging bungalows to high-density dwellings, such as apartments and condominiums, or increasing the number of school-age residents per existing household.

The latter possibility is controlled by local law. When ten victims of Hurricane Katrina were discovered by inspectors to be residing in a Manassas Park townhouse in December 2005, they were confronted with the threat of eviction (Stewart, December 10, 2005). The law requires fifty square feet per occupant in each sleeping area, which is defined as a room with a smoke detector and an emergency escape, such as a window.

When Manassas Park's neighbor, the City of Manassas, began enforcing its own overcrowding ordinance in the same month, civil rights activists publicly criticized the city for being "anti-immigrant" (McCrummen, December 28, 2005). The ordinance defined a "family" as "immediate relatives" only. Nephews and nieces, uncles and aunts, cousins, and other relatives were excluded. This provision hit the growing Hispanic population especially hard, since they frequently housed recently arrived relations until they acquired enough money to get their own residence. In the face of accusations of bigotry and threats of lawsuits by the American Civil Liberties Union, Manassas eventually suspended enforcement of the controversial ordinance, but a message still had been delivered (McCrummen, January 5, 2006). Established residents of Manassas, along with other communities with similar overcrowding laws, were clearly concerned about the influx of immigrants.

The residents of Manassas Park understood that their city's ethnic makeup was changing. While people rarely expressed fear of or disdain for recent arrivals, many wondered how changing demographics would impact the school system, social services, and the community in general.

In the fall of 2003, according to school system statistics, the enrollment of MPCS consisted of 47 percent white/not of Hispanic origin, 31 percent Hispanic, 14 percent black, and 7 percent Asian/Pacific Islander. Two years later, in the fall of 2005, the percentage of white/not of Hispanic origin students had dropped to 39 percent, the percentage of black students had dropped to 13.5 percent, and the percentage of Asian/Pacific Islanders had dropped to 6.8 percent. Hispanic enrollment, on the other hand, rose to 38 percent, nearly equaling the white enrollment. Of the 2,358 students enrolled in MPCS as of September, 2005, 589 (25%) were classified as Limited English Proficient (LEP).

When the Manassas Park leadership team met for their annual retreat in August 2004, Tom DeBolt had asked everyone to read *The Tipping Point* (2002), by Malcolm Gladwell. The book advanced the notion that substantive change can happen very rapidly once a certain momentum has built. During the discussion of the book, members of the leadership team wondered whether Manassas Park faced a demographic "tipping point." Would the makeup of the school system suddenly become predominantly Hispanic as more immigrants arrived and more longtime residents departed? What accommodations would the schools have to make in order to sustain their success during such a period of demographic change? Would there be economic consequences resulting from the growing population of recent immigrants?

Pat Miller was particularly aware of Manassas Park's changing demographics. When Cougar Elementary opened for the fall semester of 2006, the second grade was 52 percent Hispanic. The percentage of Hispanics in the other grades at Cougar exceeded 40 percent. Miller's primary concern, though, was not based on student ethnicity. Cougar's greatest educational challenge, in her estimation, was the growing transience of families. "We're never looking at the same student population in any two years at Cougar," she explained. Teachers just began to get to know students and understand their needs and family circumstances, and suddenly the students had moved to another school system.

To help the community plan for a future with a growing Hispanic population, Mayor Frank Jones and the Manassas Park City Council organized a series of Hispanic Needs Forums in late 2005 and early 2006 (Gilbert, January 26, 2006). At one forum, Jones revealed his concerns: "I'm here because I believe it is the inherent responsibility of every government to guarantee the well-being of its citizens," he declared. "My biggest fear is that the lack of understanding of the Hispanic community will lead to hatred. . . . I grew up in the deep South, and if we don't learn the lessons of the late 1960s, we will repeat the same mistakes. I will not let this happen on my watch" (p. A2).

City officials attending the forums heard Hispanic residents complain about how many bureaucratic hurdles they had to jump in order to obtain business permits. Some spoke of routine humiliations and being made fun of by non–Hispanic peers. Others addressed gaps in social services. Several teenagers admitted that their main interest in coming to the United States was to earn money, not obtain an education. In many cases, parents of young Hispanics had little formal education. Some were illiterate in their native language. Trying to convince them that their children needed to complete high school was not always easy.

If the influx of Hispanic immigrants continues, Manassas Park City Schools will have to bolster its ESL and outreach programs as well as attract more Spanish-speaking staff. In the fall of 2006 the school system took an important step by planning "Welcome Centers" for each school. Each center was designed to serve as a one-stop source of information regarding public services for Hispanic residents. Indications are that the Hispanic community will do what it can to support these and related efforts. Several well-to-do Hispanic businessmen, for example, have pledged to contribute resources and sponsor scholarships to assist Hispanic students. Also gratifying is the fact that the school system and city council have chosen to address Manassas Park's changing demographics early, when constructive action still can be taken, instead of ignoring the issue or waiting until local services are overwhelmed by unmet needs.

Earlier it was noted that Manassas Park's potential for population growth was somewhat limited by the lack of available land for new homes and apartments. This fact did not mean, however, that the school-age population would remain relatively constant. In 2006, enrollment topped 2,400 students, a new high. Cougar Elementary, with more than nine hundred students in kindergarten through third grade, faced serious overcrowding issues. The obvious solution would be to build another elementary school for the primary grades, but such a solution could also generate problems. As long as one facility serves all the primary grade students in the city, there is no possibility of social stratification by school and interschool jealousy. As soon as a second school for the same age group is built, the potential for segregation by neighborhood and claims of favoritism by parents arises. So far Manassas Park has avoided these problems because there were only four schools, an early elementary, intermediate elementary, middle, and high school.

One possible way to circumvent these problems as enrollments grow would be to build a new Manassas Park Elementary School large enough to hold Cougar's third graders. Moving third graders to Manassas Park Elementary would free up space at overcrowded Cougar, while maintaining the arrangement whereby every student of a particular age attends the same public school in Manassas Park.

WILL LOCAL REVENUE FOR EDUCATION CONTINUE TO BE ADEQUATE?

Manassas Park's milestone revenue sharing agreement clearly had been a crucial step on the road to educational excellence, but it was not a guarantee of generous resources. If local revenues plummeted, the school system's 57 percent share would have to be taken from a diminished treasury. Such a prospect seemed remote in the fall of 2005 when a flush local economy and booming housing market prompted the city council to lower the real estate tax rate to $1.25 per $100 of assessed value, a four-cent reduction (Seal, October 12, 2005). The lower rate was offset, though, by steadily rising assessments. In 2004, the average assessed value of homes in Manassas Park jumped an impressive 28 percent, the largest increase in northern Virginia.

What a difference a year can make. Housing markets can be very fickle, and by the fall of 2006, sales of new and existing homes had stalled in northern Virginia and across the country. As inventories of available homes ballooned, builders began offering a variety of special incentives in order to stimulate buyers. The Manassas Park City Council faced the unpleasant prospect of stable real estate assessments. If assessments remained the same in 2006, DeBolt anticipated a seven hundred thousand dollar revenue loss for the school system. The only way to maintain existing budget commitments would be to raise the tax rate. This option, however, seemed highly unlikely. Manassas Park, like many other communities, found itself in the midst of a taxpayers' revolt. The previous spring, in fact, several candidates had run for city council on a platform to cut taxes. Frank Jones expressed deep concern that many local residents were fed up with steadily rising costs for public schools. The word he kept hearing was "Enough!"

DeBolt knew as well as Jones did that years of rising assessments and higher tax bills had produced a disgruntled group of taxpayers, especially those on fixed incomes. In April 2006, just prior to city council elections, he made sure the candidates were invited to address the seniors at Manassas Park High School on the key issues in the election and the possible consequences of tax cuts (Stewart, April 28, 2006). DeBolt calculated that the seniors who were eligible to vote possibly could swing the election if turnout was relatively low. As DeBolt explained to a reporter covering the candidates, local elections in Manassas Park typically attracted around three hundred voters. At least sixty seniors were registered to vote, and experience indicated that they tended to show up on election day. The high school, after all, was a designated polling place. Having seniors understand that they controlled roughly 20 percent of the vote in local elections was an important lesson in the democratic process and a key element in DeBolt's political strategy.

Never one to be caught by surprise, DeBolt had been anticipating a possible cooling of the housing market as well as other economic changes for months. At the school board meeting of June 6, 2005, he had asked Jennifer Maguire to present a plan for the School Building Fund Budget for Fiscal Years 2005–2010 (School Board Minutes, June 6, 2005, p. 2). DeBolt and Maguire hoped the plan would persuade the school board to lobby the city council for authorization to borrow funds to complete the school system's capital projects. Maguire argued that any delay in building the new elementary school and finishing other projects was likely to be costly, given rising interest rates and construction costs. The prudent course of action, she contended, was to go for one large debt issuance as soon as possible rather than borrowing smaller amounts in several installments. On June 20, 2005, the school board voted unanimously to approve a plan to seek debt issuance of $33.4 million (School Board Minutes, June 20, 2005, p. 10). Whether the city council would give their consent, however, was uncertain. By the middle of 2006, cracks in the alliance between the school system and the city council were beginning to appear.

HOW LONG WILL THE POLITICAL ALLIANCE HOLD?

There was no question in the minds of individuals interviewed for this book that a linchpin of Manassas Park's transformation was the highly productive political alliance forged by Tom DeBolt and Frank Jones with the city council. Together they made certain that supportive individuals were appointed by the city council to sit on the school board. This meant getting involved in local politics to make certain that candidates friendly to the school system ran for office and were elected. For a decade the strategy worked remarkably well.

The first indication of trouble was the aforementioned appearance of candidates for the city council who wanted to cut taxes and limit the funds available to the school system. DeBolt was relieved when these individuals were defeated on election day, but he knew that others eventually would take their place. Then disagreements arose between the school board and the city council over the location of the new elementary school. Several options were presented to the public in a series of hearings in the late spring of 2006. The first option called for building a new facility for fourth and fifth graders on the site of Cougar Elementary School. This option would mean that all elementary students would be schooled at the same location, a decision that had obvious advantages related to transportation, program coordination, and administration. The second option entailed building a new facility for fourth and fifth graders on the site of the old Manassas Park Elementary School in Costello Park. The argument for the second option was largely symbolic in nature. By locating the new school in the older and less affluent section of Manassas Park, the school system would be seen as reaching out to that part of the community that wielded the least political clout. Choosing the first option, on the other hand, could be regarded as a vote of no confidence in Manassas Park's older neighborhoods. Several additional options involving the location of a new facility for preschoolers and improvements to the Parks and Recreation Department complex in Costello Park hinged, to some extent, on whether the first or second option was chosen.

Beneath the surface of the debate about where to locate the new Manassas Park Elementary School lay the issue of an increasingly stratified community. Where once there had been working-class homogeneity, there now was a city divided between aging neighborhoods of relatively low-cost housing occupied by recent immigrants and less well-to-do residents and upscale new subdivisions built on land annexed from Prince William County. One argument for the first option held that parents in the newer sections of Manassas Park might oppose sending their children, especially preschoolers, to a part of town they considered rundown and dangerous. The counterargument maintained that building the new school in the less affluent part of town could serve as a catalyst to neighborhood revitalization.

DeBolt, the school board, and the school system leadership team clearly favored the first option. So, too, did the majority of speakers who showed up for the public hearings. The mayor and some members of the city council, on the other hand, backed the second option. Relations between the city government and the school system grew increasingly strained over the matter. Technically speaking, the decision on where to locate a school resided with the school board, but the city council still controlled the pursestrings. If they were so inclined, they could refuse to support borrowing money to build the new school.

Indecision regarding where to locate Manassas Park Elementary School dragged on throughout the summer of 2006. Finally, in October the impasse was resolved when Mayor Frank Jones recommended that the school system give up its claim to Costello Park, thereby freeing the city to construct a "world-class" Parks and Recreation facility in the oldest section of Manassas Park. This move freed the school system to build the new elementary school adjacent to Cougar Elementary School. Because Cougar was bursting at the seams by the fall of 2006, the original plans for the new school were modified. Instead of a two-story facility housing grades four and five, the new Manassas Park Elementary School would rise to three stories and include grades three, four, and five. Cougar would lose a grade, thereby relieving overcrowding. The school system breathed a collective sigh of relief. The alliance had held, at least for the moment.

WILL STUDENT ACHIEVEMENT CONTINUE TO IMPROVE?

During Tom DeBolt's first ten years as superintendent, Manassas Park residents willingly supported steadily increasing school system budgets and ambitious building programs because they seemed to be making a difference. Student achievement rose each year and, with it, the self-esteem of the community. Manassas Park had been good to its school system, and the school system had been good for Manassas Park. People with children moving to or within northern Virginia no longer shunned Manassas Park because of its lackluster facilities and low academic performance.

Educators, at least those with a few grey hairs, understand, however, that school system turnarounds are rarely enduring. Public support may last no longer than the publication of next year's test scores. Any decline, or perceived decline, in student performance is capable of producing questions about returns on investments. "Why are we paying our teachers so much, if students are scoring less well than they used to on state tests?" "Why did we spend all that money on world-class facilities if our kids can only get into the local community college?" These are the kinds of questions that DeBolt and the members of his leadership team heard in the middle of the night as they awaited the latest set of test scores.

When the results of state testing in the spring of 2006 were finally released at the end of the summer, educators across the Virginia held their breath. Under revised federal mandate, students in grades four, six, and seven joined third, fifth, and eighth graders in taking state tests.

Principals who had moved their strongest teachers to third, fifth, and eighth grade now worried that student test performance in the other grades would suffer. Their worries were well founded. Across Virginia, math scores for middle schoolers in the sixth and seventh grades were alarmingly low (Shapira, September 2, 2006). Statewide, only 51 percent of sixth graders and 44 percent of seventh graders passed. In Manassas Park, Liz Purcell examined her students' low math and social studies scores and wondered whether there would be any backlash in the community. Would questions be raised about the wisdom of investing millions of dollars in improving Manassas Park Middle School? Or would local residents realize that low middle school scores were pervasive across the state?

At the high school, new principal Tracy Shaver registered concern that the class of 2007 was unlikely to outperform the class of 2006. Educators understand cohort effects. They know that some groups of students, for whatever reason, are more talented than other groups of students. Shaver wondered how the community would react if his first graduating class failed to match or exceed the outstanding performance of Bruce McDade's last group of seniors.

While continuing improvement on tests occupied much of the thinking of leadership team members, teachers expressed their own set of concerns. When DeBolt convened several conversations with groups of Manassas Park teachers in 2005, he got an earful about their fears that overemphasis on test preparation risked diminishing the "educational experience" of every student. Was public education to be no more than learning enough to pass a series of standardized tests? Teachers went on record as applauding DeBolt's commitment to expand each student's awareness of music, the arts, and forensics. They agreed with him that cognitive development was enhanced by experiences that went beyond memorizing material for multiple choice tests.

DeBolt and his leadership team realized that they were walking a tightrope. They could not ignore student performance on state and other standardized tests, not with newspapers covering which schools and school systems met state and federal benchmarks and which did not. At the same time, they were unlikely to retain a talented teacher corps if their sole focus was test preparation. They remained steadfastly committed to the goal of educating well-rounded students. Nonetheless, the educational leaders of Manassas Park were ecstatic when they learned that MPCS was one of only twenty-four school divisions in Virginia to have every one of its schools meet Adequate Yearly Progress and state accreditation requirements for 2006–2007. That Manassas Park served a more diverse student population than many of the other twenty-three school divisions only made the accomplishment more significant.

WHAT WILL HAPPEN WHEN TOM DEBOLT LEAVES?

School system insiders spent an anxious spring in 2006. They watched nervously as tensions between DeBolt and the school board, on one hand, and Mayor Jones and the city council, on the other hand, escalated over the location of the new Manassas Park Elementary School. In a show of power, the city council threatened not to reappoint two school board members whose terms were ending. People wondered how DeBolt would react. Would he resign if the city council carried out its threat?

The city council wound up reappointing one of the two school board members. DeBolt was not pleased to lose the other member— one of his strongest supporters. The school board then offered DeBolt a four-year contract, which, to the relief of school system supporters, he accepted. It appeared that he would remain at the helm at least long enough to see the new elementary school completed—the last jewel in the crown.

The episode served as a wakeup call to those who seemed to assume that DeBolt would be around forever. Manassas Park officials had given little thought to succession planning. There had been too many other pressing matters to which to attend. And DeBolt had gone on record as saying that he would stay the course.

DeBolt, of course, eventually will leave office. Regardless of what happened after 2005, he will be able to take great pride in what occurred during his first decade as superintendent of Manassas Park City Schools. While no school system can be transformed singlehandedly, there is some validity to the notion that the history of Manassas Park City Schools from 1995 to 2005 is the "lengthened shadow of one man." DeBolt could only hope that his efforts to build a strong leadership team, a productive political alliance, a talented staff of professional educators, an infrastructure responsive to the needs of young people, a solid foundation of local resources to support education, a collection of first-class facilities, an impressive track record of academic and extracurricular success, and a robust organizational culture of high achievement constituted a sufficient endowment to ensure the school system's success long after his departure.

Chapter 8

Understanding the Process of School System Transformation

What does it take to turn around a low-performing school system? Interest in this question has increased substantially since the advent of state and federal measures aimed at greater educational accountability. Far more is known about the process of improving individual schools, however, than about the transformation of entire school systems. In chapter 1 the suggestion was made that systemic organizational change is multidimensional. In other words, understanding the complexities of sweeping change requires more than one perspective. Drawing on the work of Bolman and Deal in *Reframing Organizations*, four perspectives were chosen to guide the examination of Manassas Park City Schools. In this chapter, each of the four perspectives will be used as a "lens" through which to review the change process in Manassas Park.

The first perspective is political. It assumes that scarce resources, differences of opinion, and conflict are endemic to organizations. There are never enough resources to satisfy the desires of all individuals and groups that work in and are served by the organization. Students of the political perspective expect that every decision regarding a change in resource allocation or any other aspect of the status quo has the potential to create winners and losers. Rarely does organizational change result in equal benefits for all. Understanding what happened in Manassas Park from a political perspective necessitates identifying points of tension and conflict and determining if and how matters were resolved.

The next perspective to be discussed is the symbolic. According to Bolman and Deal (1997, p. 217), the symbolic perspective encompasses the culture of an organization—"the interwoven pattern of beliefs, values, practices, and artifacts that define for members who they are and how they are to do things." Culture plays a critical role in organizational change. Change invariably results in actions and decisions that can seem confusing to organization members. Anxiety and ambiguity frequently accompany the change process. Organizational culture has the potential to invest aspects of the change process with meaning, thereby allaying fears and reducing confusion.

At some point in the transformation process, changes must be made in the structure of the school system, that is, if the transformation is to be sustained. Political action can set the stage for transformation and cultural change can reinforce the need for transformation, but ultimately structural change must occur in order to create the conditions for improved teaching and learning. The structural perspective focuses on organizational building blocks, including mission and goals, policies, programs, and lines of authority. The key assumption supporting the structural perspective is that the behavior of organization members is a function, to some extent, of the organization's structure.

The fourth perspective concerns human resources—the people who work in and are served by the organization. It is assumed that people's needs are complex. They go beyond collecting a paycheck or passing a test. People need to feel valued and cared about. They want to know that what they do matters and that they are contributing to a cause greater than their own self-interest. Organizational transformation in a public school system presumably depends on balancing the aspirations and needs of organizational leaders, the local community, and the individuals expected to achieve the hard work of change.

Understanding the history of an organization, especially one such as Manassas Park City Schools that underwent a dramatic turnaround, is similar to assembling a four-part puzzle. Each part represents a different perspective, and each perspective, in turn, represents a different set of assumptions about human behavior in organizational settings. Omit any piece of the puzzle and the organization's "story" is incomplete. No perspective is necessarily more important than another, and each is linked to the others in various ways. The preceding chapters related an integrated account of Manassas Park's history. The narrative, in other words, was not interrupted to comment on which perspectives were "in play" at a particular time. The present chapter returns to the narrative in order to review and appreciate the roles played by political action, cultural change, restructuring, and human resource development in the transformation of Manassas Park City Schools.

THE POWER OF POLITICS

Change is a precarious enterprise. At any given time it is safe to assume that certain individuals and groups are benefiting from the status quo. Change, therefore, poses a potential threat to these individuals and groups. Tom DeBolt understood that anything he might try to do in order to improve Manassas Park City Schools stood a good chance of meeting resistance. As he frequently noted, he was raised in south Chicago where political savvy was a birthright. Soon after his arrival in Manassas Park, he sized up the situation and realized that meaningful improvements in the school system were impossible without better funding. Better funding, in turn, was contingent on support from the city council. For the first two decades of the school system DeBolt's predecessors had gone begging for resources to the city council only to be told that the city was poor and residents would not support increased taxes. Since the city council appointed school board members and controlled the allocation of local revenue for the school system, superintendents routinely returned from their meetings with city officials, hat in hand, with few additional resources. School board members who challenged the city council's modest support risked not being reappointed.

DeBolt's personality and value system ensured that he would not follow in his predecessors' footsteps. For one thing, he did not like bullies or being bullied. He had no intention of allowing a hostile city council to browbeat him. The courage to confront the city council came in large measure from his deep-seated commitment to serve young people. DeBolt held the strong conviction that the children of Manassas Park deserved much better than they were receiving and that the school system had a moral obligation to do everything in its power to improve facilities, hire more capable teachers and administrators, and strengthen the academic program. Not one to shirk responsibility, DeBolt realized that any challenge to the city council's grip on resources would need to begin with him.

Even the most committed advocate for education knows that little can be accomplished by a solitary leader. DeBolt was fortunate that his school board chairman, Frank Jones, shared his high hopes for the school system and his disdain for the way the school system was treated by the city council. Together they developed a political strategy that called for them to become active in the local Republican Party. In DeBolt's case, this course of action meant going against all the advice he had received from his professors. They had counseled against getting involved in local partisan politics. DeBolt, however, knew he had no choice if he wanted to effect a school system turnaround.

The more they worked within the local party structure, the more DeBolt and Jones realized that lots of citizens shared their desire to improve support for the school system. Within a few years, they not only had lobbied for the appointment of school board members who shared their vision and commitment, but they had gotten individuals supportive of education elected to the city council. A key component of DeBolt's political strategy involved having candidates for local office address high school seniors. Most of the seniors were old enough to vote. In local elections that rarely drew more than three hundred voters, fifty to sixty seniors could have a major impact on the outcome. DeBolt, of course, could not tell seniors how to vote, but he could make certain that they heard candidates explain their position on support for Manassas Park City Schools.

The organizational history of Manassas Park City Schools was told by focusing on a series of critical incidents—points at which important decisions had to be made and the fate of the school system hung in the balance. Most of these critical incidents—securing funding for Manassas Park High School and Cougar Elementary School, negotiating a revenue-sharing agreement, and determining where to locate the new Manassas Park Elementary School—necessitated political action by DeBolt and the school board. Votes on the city council had to be counted. Undecided council members had to be lobbied. Local residents had to be sold on the need for better facilities and increased funding. That DeBolt and his allies eventually prevailed offers evidence that "the politics of possibility" can preempt the "politics of pessimism" if the cause is perceived to be just.

It is one thing to wage a campaign for more resources during a time of economic growth and quite another thing to do so during a period of retrenchment. By 2006, the economy in northern Virginia had begun to cool. The decision concerning where to locate the new Manassas Park Elementary School threatened the alliance between the school system and city government. As a practitioner of *realpolitik*, DeBolt was prepared to modify his political strategy in order to achieve at least part of the desired goal. In the end, he got all of what he wanted.

In chapter 2, it was noted that the survival of all organizations, school systems included, is dependent on how well the organizations address the twin challenges of external adaptation and internal integration. In other words, an organization must ensure that it gets along with those on whom it depends for resources and support while simultaneously making certain that those within the organization remain motivated and committed to the mission. When DeBolt took over in 1995, Manassas Park City Schools found itself in the unenviable position of having to sacrifice internal integration for the sake of external adaptation. In order to appease the city council, the school system was compelled to settle for poor facilities, low salaries, the continuing prospect of meager resources, and persistent micromanagement by council members. Under such circumstances, it was virtually impossible to generate any momentum within the school system to address issues of low morale and inadequate performance. During his first decade as superintendent, DeBolt, with the help of allies such as Frank Jones and a capable leadership team, was able to correct this situation and create a school system that fit well into its external environment while simultaneously cohering internally. Such an achievement was due, in no small way, to DeBolt's willingness to "play politics."

THE IMPACT OF RE-CULTURING

When DeBolt arrived in Manassas Park, he found a fragile organizational culture characterized by low expectations and fatalism. Employees tacitly accepted the school system's status as the educational doormat of northern Virginia. The high turnover of administrators and teachers bespoke the low regard in which MPCS was held. Any plea from division officials for better funding was met by a chorus of city council criticism.

DeBolt possessed an intuitive understanding that the school system and the entire community needed to be re-cultured if Manassas Park students were to receive the quality education they deserved. He also realized that cultures, even negative ones, are not changed overnight.

In writing about the symbolic dimension of organizations, Bista and Glasman (1998, pp. 112–113) observe that it entails "interpreting experience, using symbols to capture attention, discovering and communicating a vision, and telling stores." They go on to explain that symbolic leaders provide meaning for organization members as they search for support for the organization. In the first years of his super-intendency, Tom DeBolt clearly manifested the characteristics of a symbolic leader. He seized every opportunity to invest accomplishments with symbolic meaning.

The first such accomplishment was completing the new high school. Though the initial planning for the facility was initiated by his predecessor, it took DeBolt's persistence and political skills to ensure that the project was not delayed. Once completed, the impressive new school was held up as a symbol of a new era in education for Manassas Park and an example of what could be achieved when the city council, the school board, the community, and the school system worked together.

Few people believed that DeBolt could gain approval for a new elementary school so soon after the high school project, but he pressed forward anyway, using the new high school as a basis for comparison with the city's dilapidated elementary schools. It helped that the city council by this time included a majority of school system supporters and that the local economy was flourishing. When Cougar Elementary School was finished, DeBolt had yet another visible symbol of what could be accomplished when the community and the school system worked together. Subsequent initiatives that DeBolt appropriated as symbols of success included the revenue-sharing agreement, the new wing of the high school, and the renovation of the middle school. DeBolt, his leadership team, and the school board rarely missed an opportunity to point out that the community's investments in the school system were paying dividends. Student achievement continued to improve, all schools achieved state accreditation, Manassas Park teams experienced success on their "world-class" playing fields, and increasing numbers of graduates gained admission to quality institutions of higher education.

Symbols of success are a critical component of any effort to re-culture an organization. So, too, are ceremonies and rituals. No sooner had DeBolt arrived on the scene than he replicated the Celebration of Excellence ceremony that he had initiated at Pulaski High School. Other rituals, including Senior Day and the division-wide Convocation to kick off each new school year, soon followed. Each time a new building project began, a community groundbreaking ceremony was held. When a new facility was completed, school was canceled and teachers, students, and community volunteers joined in the process of moving furniture, files, and instructional materials. When the high school held its annual graduation ceremony, care was taken to invite elementary and middle school teachers. If ever there was an individual who believed in the maxim that it takes a community to raise a child, it was Tom DeBolt.

The result of these and other efforts was the replacement of the school system's previous culture of despair, defeatism, and disappointment with a robust new culture of high achievement. By 2004, the school system no longer settled for being as good as its neighbors. When the leadership team crafted a statement of shared beliefs, the first belief was "all things are possible." The accompanying vision statement—"To foster a learning community inspiring competence, confidence, and commitment"—reinforced the necessity of teamwork for achieving the school system's lofty ambitions.

The willingness of Tom DeBolt and Frank Jones to become active in local politics had generated the resources needed to transform Manassas Park City Schools, but resources alone were insufficient. A number of urban school systems have been the beneficiaries of large infusions of resources without achieving significant improvements. Re-culturing Manassas Park City Schools provided a solid foundation for sustained success. A host of symbols, rituals, shared beliefs, and expectations served to remind everyone connected to the school system that high achievement was the objective and that it was achievable.

In their efforts to re-culture the school system, DeBolt and his colleagues did have one advantage over many other low-performing school systems. The school system was young. There was no prior period—so-called glory days—when the school system had been known for providing an outstanding education. As a consequence, residents had no model of past success against which to compare what the school system was trying to accomplish. With no nostalgic attachment to bygone days, Manassas Park residents were relatively free to embrace the changes undertaken by the DeBolt administration.

THE NECESSITY OF STRUCTURE

Political action can set the stage for organizational transformation, and constructing new facilities and initiating new rituals and ceremonies can symbolize the spirit behind school system transformation, but until organizational processes, programs, policies, and practices change, transformation is likely to remain more rhetoric than reality. These changes represent structural alterations that impact what organization members strive to accomplish and how they go about accomplishing it. Structural change affects rules, roles, and relationships.

The single most important structural change in Manassas Park's transformation probably was the revenue-sharing agreement between the school board and the city council. The agreement ensured that the relationship between the local governing body and Manassas Park City Schools would not revert to what it had been prior to Tom DeBolt's arrival. For the school system's first two decades, the local resources available for public education remained a mystery that only the city council was allowed to solve. Council members used their control over resources to intimidate teachers and administrators, micromanage matters that should have been left to the school board and educators to decide, and prevent the school system from rising above mediocrity or worse. Once the revenue sharing agreement was in place, annual maneuvering and haggling over local education funds largely disappeared. DeBolt and his leadership team were free to go about the yearly business of building a budget without fear that some council member with an ax to grind would hold the budget hostage and play eleventh-hour politics with the welfare of Manassas Park youth.

Another key structural change involved the development of a long-range plan and mission statement. In some school systems, these documents serve purely symbolic purposes, but in Manassas Park the long-range plan and mission statement constituted a road map to which the leadership team frequently referred. No one familiar with these documents could doubt the direction in which Manassas Park was headed. Top-notch facilities and state of the art technology. An educational program that promised Manassas Park students opportunities to achieve anything to which they were willing to apply themselves. A commitment to develop well-rounded students who enjoyed participating in extracurricular activities and contributing to the betterment of their community.

Besides these broad aims, the long-range plan included very specific targets such as the percentage of students that would pass particular state tests and enter four-year colleges after graduation. Each year progress toward meeting the plan's objectives was reviewed. If an objective was not met, an effort was made to understand why, and corrective actions were determined. This kind of quality control and planning had not been an integral part of school system operations prior to DeBolt's arrival. If specific objectives did exist, they were not widely known nor used to guide day-to-day operations.

The role of the superintendent's lieutenants took on much greater significance after 1995. Prior to that time, several factors served to marginalize the influence of central office administrators and building principals. First, they had to contend with the micromanagerial predilections of the city council. Second, the turnover among school system administrators was so great that the stability necessary for a leadership team to operate effectively was absent. After DeBolt's arrival, things began to change. Administrators committed to DeBolt's vision were recruited and retained. The leadership team became a key component of Manassas Park's authority structure. As trust among leadership team members grew, DeBolt shared an increasing number of responsibilities with the team, including planning, staff development, troubleshooting, and strategizing. By 2005 there were very few issues facing the school system that were not addressed and vetted by the leadership team.

Many of the structural changes that had the most direct impact on teaching and learning occurred at the school level. While most elementary schools in Virginia and across the country persisted with an organizational structure based largely on self-contained classes with one teacher handling virtually all academic instruction for fifteen to thirty students, Cougar Elementary School adopted a more complex departmentalized arrangement in which students moved from classroom to classroom during the day. Instruction in technology, science, and social studies was handled by teacher specialists working in specially equipped centers. Manassas Park educators believed that young students benefited from the exposure to multiple instructors in varied settings.

Some of the most consequential structural changes involved the daily schedule. Before Tom DeBolt ever came to Manassas Park, he was convinced of the value of a block schedule for secondary students. Instead of a traditional schedule in which students met with each teacher for a relatively short "period" every day, the block schedule entailed fewer classes for longer amounts of time. Instead of six or seven classes each day, students took three or four, thereby allowing them to concentrate their energies and reducing the number of students with whom each teacher had daily contact. The block schedule was especially helpful for students who needed extra time to grasp difficult material. Both Manassas Park Middle School and Manassas Park High School adopted the block schedule.

While the block schedule was not unusual in secondary schools, it was relatively rare at the elementary level. Schools organized around self-contained classes did not require sophisticated scheduling. When Cougar and Manassas Park Elementary opted for forms of departmentalization that required students to move from one teacher to another at various points in the day, a variation of the block schedule was chosen. This schedule provided the necessary flexibility to allow struggling students to receive more instruction in core content areas than their peers. Students who did not require additional time were presented with instructional options and enrichment opportunities.

With the advent of a new state testing program in 1998, Manassas Park administrators realized that coordination between teachers was more essential than ever. The success of students at each grade level was contingent on how well they had been prepared at the previous grade levels. Poor coverage of curriculum content in one class increased the likelihood that students would struggle in subsequent classes. To reduce the possibility of such problems, Manassas Park principals arranged for teachers to meet in horizontal and vertical teams. Horizontal teams represented all the teachers who worked with students in a given grade. By meeting regularly, these teachers made certain they were moving forward together, covering the same basic content, and identifying students who needed extra help. Vertical teams involved teachers from different grade levels who handled the same subject matter. By meeting periodically, these teachers ensured that students received the necessary prerequisites before moving on to tackle more advanced material. Vertical teaming was not limited to teachers in the same school. Taking advantage of Manassas Park's small size, principals periodically arranged for teachers from different schools to meet and discuss matters of common concern. Some Cougar teachers even engaged in looping, an arrangement in which they followed a group of students from one grade to another. Looping ensured that teachers who understood the idiosyncratic needs of their students continued to use their knowledge to customize instruction.

Structural changes of the kinds noted above constitute examples of what some organization theorists (Adler & Borys, 1996; Hoy &

Sweetland, 2001) refer to as "enabling bureaucracy." In contrast to the conventional notion of bureaucratic structure as a constraint on organization members, their research suggests that, under certain conditions, it can enhance satisfaction, increase innovation, reduce role conflict, and lessen feelings of alienation (Hoy & Sweeetland, 2001, p. 297). The organizational history of Manassas Park City Schools between 1995 and 2005 suggests that Tom DeBolt and the members of his leadership team possessed an understanding of this possibility and found ways for the structure of the school system and the four schools to enhance rather than inhibit the work of professional educators.

THE POTENTIAL OF PEOPLE

The point has been made so often that it hardly seems necessary to repeat it—organizations do not change unless the people in the organizations change (Duke, 2004; Hall & Hord, 2001). Some school systems, however, continue to attempt substantive reform solely by restructuring, realigning, and reorganizing. The success of Manassas Park's transformation can be traced, to a great extent, to the fact that Tom DeBolt recognized the importance of individual as well as organizational change. He also appreciated the fact that individuals are more likely to embrace change when they feel valued and when their needs are not minimized.

William Bridges (2004) has drawn a useful distinction between "change" and "transition." Change is situational; transition is psychological. An individual changes when he moves to a new location or takes on a new job. Without transition, however, he may remain the same person as before, with the same beliefs, attitudes, and expectations, despite relocating or tackling a new role. Transition, to Bridges, represents an individual's "inner reorientation and self-redefinition" that must be experienced in order to successfully accommodate change (p. xii).

Tom DeBolt was unfamiliar with Bridges's work, but he understood that Manassas Park City Schools could not be transformed as an organization until teachers and administrators experienced a shift in their mindset. They needed to believe in themselves and their capacity for making a demonstrable difference in the lives of students. The acquisition of confidence and a sense of professional efficacy depended on a number of factors, including skill development, teamwork, and a willingness to abandon the search for excuses. In the case of some individuals, DeBolt determined that they were unlikely ever to achieve such transition and would need to be replaced. Those who embraced transition, on the other hand, deserved to be rewarded appropriately for their efforts.

A key component of DeBolt's transformation plan involved improving the salaries of all school system employees, from principals and teachers to custodians and bus drivers. He and the school board realized that improving the quality of education for Manassas Park students depended on the talents of teachers, the leadership of school administrators, and the dedication of support staff. Capable people might be recruited by appealing to their sense of mission, but retaining them ultimately was contingent on what they earned and how they were treated. During his first decade in office, DeBolt and his allies on the school board and city council managed to raise professional salaries from among northern Virginia's lowest to among the highest. Teachers, administrators, and other staff members got the message that they were important. Turnover, especially among administrators, plummeted.

There is more to job satisfaction, of course, than money. To feel valued, individuals need to know that their opinions matter. People appreciate recognition and opportunities to exercise leadership. They need to feel that what they do matters.

Manassas Park educators had no trouble realizing that what they were doing mattered. Each year they saw the pass rate on standardized tests climb. They took pride in the growing percentage of students who enrolled in higher education programs after graduation. They delighted in the fact that large numbers of recent immigrants acquired the knowledge and skills to succeed in school and in life. They celebrated when their schools achieved state accreditation and Annual Yearly Progress. They cheered as their students excelled in athletics, forensics, and the performing arts.

DeBolt and the leadership team made certain that staff members were recognized for their contributions to student success. That is why Bruce McDade made certain that all teachers, not just high school teachers, were invited to high school graduation. That is why Tom DeBolt insisted that all employees of the school system, not just certificated staff, gathered for the annual Convocation. That is why Ritchie Carroll acknowledged teachers who achieved continuing contract status by presenting them to the school board and giving them a plaque.

The belief that undergirded Manassas Park's approach to "human resources" was that school system employees should think of themselves as professionals and be treated accordingly. Being a professional meant accepting responsibility for one's role in achieving the organization's mission, being accountable for one's actions, and continuing to refine one's skills and knowledge. Those who manifested these qualities clearly "fit" the new image of a Manassas Park City Schools staff member. Those who did not manifest these qualities were counseled to find work elsewhere.

In return for conducting themselves as professionals, employees were accorded the respect befitting a professional. Teachers were provided with attractive and well-appointed office space in each of the new schools. Coaches enjoyed offices and facilities that were the envy of their peers in other school systems. Opportunities for staff development were abundant, and support for work on advanced degrees was generous. Classified personnel also were provided with inservice training, and care was taken to hold their training sessions at attractive locations. Teachers and administrators were encouraged to attend conferences at division expense and become active in professional associations.

Professionals presumably possess expertise that renders their opinions and judgments relevant. Respect for the "voice" of professionals should begin at the top of the organization, and so it did in Manassas Park. When DeBolt arrived, the days of teachers and administrators getting browbeaten by city officials were numbered. DeBolt modeled high regard for his leadership team by seeking their counsel on practically every matter of significance. Leadership team members, in turn, frequently tapped the wisdom of their staffs. When DeBolt felt he might be "losing touch" with the "front lines," he arranged for "conversations" with groups of teachers. When Gail Pope wanted to know how to identify the best new candidates for teaching positions, she gathered the top teachers in the school system and asked them what to look for. No new facility in Manassas Park was planned without teachers being consulted for their design ideas.

Manassas Park administrators are enamored of the notion of a professional learning community, a group of educators committed to common goals who work and learn together on a continuing basis. Members of a professional learning community are not hung up on titles and roles. They are willing to acknowledge when they have a problem and when they need to increase their knowledge in order to be more effective. To a great extent the leadership team functions in this manner, and it is the desire of team members that eventually the entire school system will do likewise.

A SYSTEMATIC APPROACH TO SYSTEMIC CHANGE

Much is made of the necessity for systemic change in low-performing school systems. Advocates of systemic change note that the various functions involved in providing young people with an education are inseparable. Tinkering with one aspect of schooling without appreciating its connection to the entire enterprise is a sure way to short-circuit improvement efforts. California politicians learned this lesson the hard way when they approved a bill to lower class size in the early elementary grades. Lower class sizes meant that each school had to increase the number of classrooms available for instruction. Many schools already were overcrowded, which meant that there was no place to put extra classes. To make matters worse, there were not enough teachers available to provide instruction in the additional classes.

School systems in California eventually added enough new classrooms and hired enough new teachers to meet the class size mandate. Systemic change of a sort was achieved, but not in a very systematic way. Achieving systemic change in a systematic way requires careful planning and forethought. Thinking in advance about the impact of change and the resources needed to achieve change minimizes the potential disruptive effects of change. Such disruptions have undermined more than one large-scale effort to improve schooling.

By looking at the organizational history of Manassas Park City Schools in terms of Bolman and Deal's four perspectives, it becomes abundantly clear that systemic change was achieved in a relatively systematic way. Tom DeBolt and the school board appreciated the relationship between student achievement, teacher compensation, school facilities, and school leadership. They understood the connection between improved educational practice, symbolism, and changes in organizational culture. They recognized the importance of community support for and involvement in the change process. They grasped the necessity of political action to achieve their aims. By making certain that virtually all students benefited from their actions, DeBolt and the school board ensured that conflict and political turmoil would be minimal. The transformation of Manassas Park City Schools had few, if any, "losers." Perhaps the greatest testament to the success of the school system's turnaround was the total absence of public and professional calls for a return to "the way things used to be."

Chapter 9

The Significance of
Manassas Park's Transformation

Organizational histories are not just interesting stories of struggles and successes in organizational settings. They provide important lessons for groups facing various internal and external challenges. Sometimes an organizational history can dampen hopes and dispirit those striving to overcome these challenges. In other cases, such as the recent history of Manassas Park City Schools, the message is uplifting, especially for educators in urban settings working with limited resources and a diverse population. An organizational history enables the reader not only to understand the antecedents and consequences of change, but also to appreciate how particular changes actually take place. Under the lens of the organizational historian, change becomes a process, not simply an isolated occasion. The process typically is ongoing, as shifting circumstances intervene to alter original intentions. We see how initiatives designed to address a particular concern evolve over time.

Transformational change of the kind experienced by Manassas Park City Schools actually involves a multitude of changes, some anticipated, others not. Seeing how these separate changes affect each other is one great benefit of organizational history. Another benefit concerns the attention given to context, both temporal and geographic. It would be impossible to grasp the full significance of the Manassas Park City Schools' story, for example, without knowing something about the region where Manassas Park is located, the nature of the community itself, and the "times" during which the transformation took place. It is of no small consequence, for example, that Manassas

143

Park is surrounded by affluent and high-performing school systems, that it once was regarded as a relatively poor community with a low-performing school system, and that the period between 1995 and 2005 was one in which large-scale educational accountability initiatives were launched at the state and federal levels.

In this concluding chapter, several "lessons" from the organizational history of Manassas Park City Schools are identified and discussed. The first lesson is that low-performing school systems need not resign themselves to being educational backwaters. Much can be done to overcome the conditions that undermine academic success. The second and third lessons concern the change process itself. Manassas Park City Schools under Tom DeBolt's leadership undertook improvements in a way that can best be described as "accelerating incrementalism." One hallmark of the change process in Manassas Park was the avoidance of conspicuous labels for reforms and the wholesale importation of "packaged" improvement programs.

The next four lessons address crucial components of Manassas Park's transformation. That Manassas Park City Schools enjoyed a manageable size, unlike many large urban school systems, cannot be ignored. Nor can the importance of improving the facilities in which teachers teach and students learn. Broad-based community support was a third element in the formula that led to academic success. The fourth and perhaps most important ingredient in Manassas Park's success was leadership, especially the leadership of Tom DeBolt, but also the leadership of Frank Jones and the school board, key figures in the central office, and principals. The last lesson of the Manassas Park story concerns the role that school system transformation can play in community transformation. It is clear that the emergence of Manassas Park as a desirable place to live and raise a family was attributable, in no small way, to the school system's turnaround.

LESSON 1: SCHOOL SYSTEMS CAN BE TURNED AROUND

Much of the focus of educational reform in the eighties and nineties was school improvement. While many of these efforts yielded remarkable results, others only produced disappointment and frustration. Educators and policymakers came to realize that improving schools depended a great deal on school system support. When the school system was unhealthy, the prognosis for individual schools was often unfavorable. In

2002 Harvard University launched the Public Education Leadership Project in order to shift the focus of reform from schools to school systems. An article on the project in the *Harvard Business Review* (Childress, Elmore, & Grossman, 2006, p. 55) underscored the necessity of addressing school improvement systemically:

> School-based solutions, while important, aren't enough. If they were, and low-performing schools could heal themselves, urban systems today would be chock-full of highly functioning schools. Achieving excellence on a broad scale requires a districtwide strategy for improving instruction in the classroom and an organization that can implement it. Only the district office can create such a plan, identify and spread best practices, develop leadership capabilities at all levels, build information systems to monitor student improvement, and hold people accountable for results.

Saying that a school system needs to be transformed is one thing, and actually accomplishing such a feat is quite another. As McLaughlin and Talbert (2002, p. 187) observe, "Conventional wisdom holds that districts cannot undertake or sustain serious reform." They go on to note three reasons for the failure of many system-wide improvement efforts: "school-level resistance to a strong central office role, personnel turnover, and the politics of local education reform." As the organizational history of Manassas Park City Schools has demonstrated, however, each of these challenges can be addressed successfully.

Hope and public education, especially for the neediest students, are inextricably linked. If public schools offered no hope for a better life for individuals and a better overall society, there would be little reason to support such institutions. The demonstrated success of Manassas Park City Schools in overcoming underfunding, mismanagement, lack of leadership, inadequate facilities, and low academic achievement offers hope to those on whose shoulders rest the hopes of millions of students stuck in circumstances similar to those that greeted Tom DeBolt when he assumed the superintendency. Manassas Park City Schools, of course, is not the only school system to reverse the downward spiral of low performance. Its transformation, however, has been studied sufficiently to provide relatively clear guidance to communities and educators desiring to effect comparable "miracles." As Ron Edmunds noted three decades ago, the value of a positive example is immense. When at least one low-performing school system is able to achieve comprehensive improvements, the excuse that such an accomplishment is impossible no longer is tenable.

Some critics of contemporary efforts to improve public education register concern that there is too much emphasis these days on raising scores on standardized tests (Kohn, 1999; Ohanian, 1999). They worry that students will become mere numbers to be aggregated and disaggregated for accountability purposes. One of the most impressive features of Manassas Park's transformation has been the school system's ability to raise test scores without sacrificing the development of well-rounded students. Manassas Park educators have demonstrated that the so-called "basics" can be attended to while expanding opportunities for students to engage in enriching academic experiences and extracurricular activities.

LESSON 2: A CHANGE PROCESS CHARACTERIZED BY ACCELERATING INCREMENTALISM

In thinking about organizational change, theorists have tried to account for three aspects of change: what is changed, the consequences of change, and how change is achieved (Duke, 2004, pp. 235–256). The Manassas Park story offers particular insight into the last aspect—the process by which organizational transformation is achieved.

Before discussing this process, it may be helpful to reflect on several ways that organizational change has been characterized in the literature. One popular approach involves the distinction between evolutionary and revolutionary or radical change. Evolutionary change—sometimes referred to as incrementalism—proceeds in a steady but nondramatic way (Duke, 2004, p. 242; Lindblom, 1980). Progress is made without a sharp and tumultuous break with the status quo. Continuity is the hallmark of evolutionary change.

Critics of evolutionary change, going back to Karl Marx, argue that it ensures the perpetuation of the existing order. Incremental improvements mollify the discontented without displacing the power structure or threatening those who have benefited from the status quo. Only radical change, from this perspective, has the potential to produce a qualitative shift in organizational outcomes.

One of the most thoroughly studied attempts to effect radical change in a school system involved the efforts of Superintendent Alan Bersin and his chancellor of instruction, Anthony Alvarado, to "jolt" the San Diego City Schools (Hightower, 2002). Bersin previously served as the U.S. Attorney for the Southern District of California, a position in which he had distinguished himself as a champion of equity and social justice. Alvarado had been the superintendent of New York City's Community School District #2, a role in which he gained national recognition for achieving system-wide instructional improvement. Together they undertook a program of sweeping reforms designed to quickly correct the ill effects of years of decentralization and lack of academic focus. The central administration was decimated in order to free up resources for instructional improvement at the school level. Personnel that could not justify their roles in terms of contributions to improved teaching and learning found themselves looking for employment elsewhere. Budgets were reconfigured to reflect the central importance of instructional needs. In reflecting on his first months in office, Bersin concluded:

> There was no other way to start systemic reform. You don't announce it. You've got to jolt the system. I understood that. You've got to jolt a system, and if people don't understand you're serious about change in the first 6 months, the bureaucracy will own you. The bureaucracy will defeat you at every turn if you give it a chance. (Hightower, 2002, p. 80)

Under Bersin and Alvarado's leadership, the quality of instruction at the elementary level began to improve. Principals started to function as instructional leaders, and teachers received continuous staff development focused on raising student achievement through careful alignment of teaching, curriculum standards, and assessment. These early accomplishments came at a significant cost, however. Bersin and Alvarado angered the teachers union and upset high school educators who felt standardized approaches to reform were ill-suited to secondary education. Bersin and Alvarado also disagreed on certain strategic matters, ultimately resulting in Alvarado's departure. Eventually Bersin, too, was compelled to leave, his grand design only partially implemented.

Tom DeBolt may have felt that Manassas Park needed a jolt, but his approach to organizational change was less radical than Bersin and

Alvarado's. Perhaps he knew that the community was not ready for an overnight revolution. Or possibly his change strategy was not fully developed in advance, only emerging slowly as he assessed his resources and support. DeBolt clearly lacked sufficient talent on staff when he first took over to accomplish systemic change. Whatever his reasoning, DeBolt's approach initially followed the path of incrementalism. Over time, however, the pace of change picked up as Manassas Park educators and community members saw the benefits of early improvements and learned to trust the motives of school system leaders. Consequently, it may be more accurate to characterize the process of organizational change in Manassas Park City Schools between 1995 and 2005 as "accelerating incrementalism." In other words, as confidence in and support for school system initiatives increased, so, too, did the pace of change. Nowhere was this process more apparent than school facilities. It took DeBolt's predecessors years to make the case for at least one new school. Once the high school was built and people realized how it enhanced learning, community pride, and real estate values, DeBolt was able to press ahead in a surprisingly brief period of time with a new lower elementary school, an addition to the high school, and a renovated middle school. Plans for a new upper elementary school—the last piece of the puzzle—were approved as this book was being completed.

San Diego and Manassas Park are hardly comparable, so it is by no means clear whether "accelerating incrementalism" would have been a better change strategy for Bersin and Alvarado. What "accelerating incrementalism" allowed DeBolt to do, however, was to mobilize political support and build a cadre of leaders and talented teachers capable of achieving school system transformation. In hindsight, the approach appears to have been very effective.

A theory of change that has attracted some attention in recent years is punctuated equilibrium theory (Romanelli & Tushman, 1994). This theory, as applied to organizations, holds that organizations go through long periods of stability (equilibrium) during which relatively little change occurs. These periods are punctuated by "short bursts" of fundamental change. One day observers may look back on the first decade of Tom DeBolt's superintendency as such a "short burst" of major organizational change. What might seem, in other words, to have been a relatively protracted period of "accelerating incrementalism" in the thirty years of Manassas Park's brief existence eventually could be reinterpreted as a brief, almost radical transformation. Our interpretation of change, as in so many other areas of inquiry, invariably is affected by our temporal distance from the events in question.

LESSON 3: SCHOOL SYSTEM CHANGE BENEFITS FROM LOCAL ADAPTATION

Public schools and school systems since the 1970s have been targeted for an array of packaged programs and highly prescriptive reforms. Ranging from sets of principles to which educators are supposed to commit themselves to comprehensive initiatives encompassing teaching strategies, curriculum materials, and organizational guidelines, these efforts to improve education frequently are designed to minimize the likelihood of local "tinkering." Proponents of particular programs and reforms contend that their effectiveness depends on implementing exactly what the designers intended. Deviating from the prototype, they argue, increases the possibility of unsuccessful change.

The literature on educational change includes examples where the wholesale importation of reforms has worked well and where it has failed (Bodilly, 1996; Duke, 2004; Muncey & McQuillan, 1996). When a Rand researcher reviewed a number of school improvement efforts, she concluded that the chances of successful reform were greatest when the change process was characterized by "mutual adaptation" (McLaughlin, 1990). Reforms imported from external sources into schools and school systems, in other words, benefited from a process of fitting the reforms to local circumstances without sacrificing their essential character.

Manassas Park's approach to school-based and system-wide improvement between 1995 and 2005 closely resembled the Rand recommendation. Whether it was a new school schedule or an approach to literacy, Manassas Park educators insisted on adapting reforms to local circumstances. Advice from teachers and other staff members typically was sought, both prior to adoption and after implementation. Parents and students also were provided opportunities to provide input on a number of new initiatives. While Manassas Park's transformation is not a fairy tale in which everyone always got exactly what they hoped for, few individuals could claim that they were not given a chance to air their feelings about proposed changes.

It is interesting to contrast Manassas Park's experience with that of Cottonwood (a pseudonym) School District, as described in

Brouillette's *A Geology of School Reform* (1996). Cottonwood undertook
a number of highly publicized and extensive reforms, including mastery
learning, shared decision making, and management by objectives. In most
cases, Cottonwood administrators tried to implement the reforms much
as external designers had intended. Little evidence of "mutual adaptation"
was reported. No sooner was a new initiative announced by the central
administration than it became a target for public debate and resistance.

     Besides his commitment to staff and community "buy-in" to re-
form and his belief that all imported programs and ideas must be
adapted to local circumstances, Tom DeBolt also understood the benefit
of not giving reforms a highly publicized label. Labels quickly become
targets for opponents and opportunities for misunderstanding. Unlike
Cottonwood, improvement efforts in Manassas Park, with the exception of new school construction, rarely received a great deal of district-
sponsored publicity. Buzzwords and bold claims were kept to a minimum.
Many of the reforms that were introduced between 1995 and 2005
were either homegrown or characterized by substantial local modification.

LESSON 4: SIZE PROBABLY MATTERS

When people think of city school systems, huge districts such as New
York City and Los Angeles probably come to mind. There are more
students in some New York City high schools, in fact, than there are
in the entire Manassas Park school system. While MPCS has had to deal
with issues such as increasing student diversity and uncertain funding
that are common to large urban school districts, differences in the scale
and scope of the issues make direct comparisons unwise. It is worth
noting, however, that many large school systems have found it necessary
to subdivide into more manageable units (Jones, 2006).

     One way to think about the basic organizational unit of a school
system is to begin with a high school, typically the largest school
organization in a district, and add the middle school or schools that
send students to the high school and the elementary school or schools
that send students to the middle school(s). This arrangement is often
referred to as a "feeder system," and it can be regarded as the fundamental unit of collective educational accountability. In other words, the
success of the high school is dependent on what is learned in the
middle school, which in turn depends on what is learned in the elementary school.

Manassas Park City Schools constitutes a single feeder system—Cougar Elementary sends students to Manassas Park Elementary which sends students to Manassas Park Middle School which sends students to Manassas Park High School. Competition and insidious comparisons between schools are eliminated because there is only one school for each age group. It is unlikely that Manassas Park's transformation would have progressed as well as it did had Tom DeBolt and his leadership team been compelled to deal with multiple schools at each level. One reason why Bersin and Alvarado's plan to transform education in San Diego ran into trouble was the contention of educators at certain high schools in affluent neighborhoods that their needs were different from other San Diego high schools (Darling-Hammond et al., 2003). Interschool jealousies and cross-grade coordination problems are minimized when there is a single feeder system with a single school at each level. The matter of building a new school, for example, can become enormously complex when some students get to attend the new facility while others of the same age are compelled to attend older and possibly less well-equipped facilities.

It may be unrealistic to think of replacing large urban school systems with a collection of "neighborhood" school systems the size of Manassas Park, but it is not unreasonable to imagine reorganizing such large systems along the lines of feeder systems. Efforts to effect improvements in a huge urban school district may be facilitated by undertaking reforms on a feeder system rather than a system-wide basis. Educators and community members are more likely, it can be argued, to develop loyalty to and identification with a feeder system than with an entire district with hundreds of schools.

LESSON 5: DON'T UNDERESTIMATE THE IMPORTANCE OF IMPROVED FACILITIES

It is tempting to believe that teaching and learning can occur anywhere. Young Abe Lincoln, after all, studied in front of a fireplace in a log cabin. Researchers have been hard-pressed to offer conclusive evidence that the quality of school facilities is related to student achievement (Duke, 1998). Students cannot be randomly assigned to different learning environments for research purposes, and, even if they could, there are so many variables potentially affecting learning that isolating the effect of physical space would be very difficult.

Despite these reservations, the fact still remains that student achievement in Manassas Park began to improve following the completion of the new high school and Cougar Elementary School. While many factors doubtless contributed to these gains, it is impossible to rule out the positive influence of new facilities. All the new schools in Manassas Park were designed with optimal learning in mind. Noisy activities are physically separated from those requiring quiet. All new schools are equipped with the latest wireless technology and state-of-the-art science labs. Each new school boasts room arrangements intended to facilitate team teaching. Each school includes attractive work space for teachers and an inviting media center for students. Even the sites on which the schools sit are landscaped to complement the facilities and provide outdoor learning environments.

Some of the benefits of improved school facilities involve intangibles. Students express great pride in their "world-class" schools. No longer are they embarrassed to host athletic contests or entertain students from other school systems. Pride of place is manifested in the absence of litter and graffiti. Manassas Park residents are pleased with the national recognition that their schools have earned. They are glad that the days of leaky roofs and undulating flooring are over. When educators are distracted by problems with facilities and school system resources must be diverted to shore up deteriorating buildings, it cannot help but have an adverse effect on teaching and learning. Manassas Park teachers and students today are free to concentrate on the education process.

LESSON 6: THE NECESSITY OF BROAD-BASED COMMUNITY SUPPORT

In their examination of reforms in large urban school systems, Hill, Campbell, and Harvey (2000, p. 106) conclude, "For a reform strategy to survive, its leaders must build as broad a coalition as is consistent with a focused initiative and either channel opposition in productive ways or meet it with countervailing ideas, organization, and political pressure." Tom DeBolt and Frank Jones clearly grasped the necessity of coalition building and countering the opposition of city council members who balked at investing in Manassas Park City Schools. They knew that replacing "regressives" with "progressives" on the city council required mobilizing community support and direct political action. Support was needed from all segments of the population. In order to gain such widespread support, DeBolt and his leadership team made certain that their proposed changes benefited as many students as possible. If improvements were undertaken for athletic facilities, there was also an effort made to enhance the music program. Programs for at-risk students were balanced by expanded opportunities for gifted students.

Without broad-based community support, achieving the transformation of Manassas Park City Schools would have been impossible. Local taxpayers had to be willing to ante up for new facilities and higher salaries. Parents had to endorse changes in academic emphasis, new school schedules, and alterations in school organization. Successful members of the growing Hispanic community had to become active in the schools. In order to generate this level of support, DeBolt, Jones, and others needed to adopt a mindset that regarded the community as more than just a *context* for change (Marsh, 2002, p. 38). Community members had to have opportunities to become *actors* in the change process.

Between 1995 and 2005 there were many such opportunities. DeBolt and Jones scheduled public hearings whenever they anticipated controversy over a proposed change. Public hearings were instrumental, for example, in determining where the new Manassas Park Elementary School would be located. Special forums were important for conveying to the Hispanic community the city's interest in and commitment to addressing their concerns. When parents expressed their concerns, school officials made certain that they followed up. DeBolt used occasions such as the groundbreakings for new schools and their subsequent dedications to thank the community for its generosity and support. Each principal encouraged faculty and students to find ways to give back to Manassas Park by means of charitable endeavors and public service.

LESSON 7: TRANSFORMATION STARTS AT THE TOP

As word of Manassas Park's success spread, Tom DeBolt received requests to speak about the school system's transformation. He prepared a PowerPoint presentation entitled "The Cornerstone of Our Success" in which he identified ten key factors. They included the following items:

1. Outstanding support and leadership from the Manassas Park School Board and the strong support of the City Governing Body and other community Leaders

2. Significantly increasing the investment in education by the City of Manassas Park and involving the community to promote ownership

3. Selecting the finest educational professionals and support staff members

4. Significant improvements to salaries, benefits, and staff development

5. Restructuring and reorganizing the way we use time

6. Strengthening the K-12 Reading program and designing and implementing curriculum based on the Standards of Learning

7. Supporting the educational program with large infusions of instructional material and technology

8. Expanding and strengthening the K-12 Fine Arts and student activities programs

9. Significantly improving our school facilities

10. Implementing strong fiscal management and continuously improving our business practices

The organizational history of Manassas Park City Schools bears out the importance of each of DeBolt's ten elements of success, but one element is conspicuously absent. Given DeBolt's modesty, he would never cite himself, but virtually everyone else connected to the school system has little doubt that there would have been no transformation without DeBolt's dynamic leadership. What specifically is it about his leadership that made such a difference?

DeBolt is, in many ways, a traditionalist. He believes in school spirit, professionalism, and the mission of public education. At the same time, he is not afraid to challenge sacred assumptions and question conventional practice. His willingness to set aside nonpartisanship and become active in local politics has been noted. While many of his peers reluctantly focused exclusively on raising test scores, DeBolt insisted on balancing this concern with improvements in extracurricular opportunities and the fine arts. He understands that a diet of standardized tests is insufficient to nourish the hearts and minds of young people. While many elementary educators clung to the time-honored self-contained classroom as the foundation for elementary school organization, DeBolt embraced a departmental model in which students were exposed each day to various teacher specialists. When it came to building new schools, DeBolt was one of the first superintendents in Virginia to adopt the construction management approach whereby the school system served as the general contractor. This decision meant that more of his time had to be devoted to monitoring building projects, but the savings were appreciable.

To say that DeBolt possessed a vision of what Manassas Park and its school system could be is to risk understatement. Nothing less than a world-class education for every student would satisfy him. Unlike many visionaries, however, he was able to keep one eye on the horizon and the other eye on the ground. When a leader's gaze is fixed on the future, it is easy to stumble and fall over seemingly minor bumps in the road. DeBolt never allowed his dreams to obscure his next steps. He made a point of listening to critics as well as supporters, thereby avoiding unpleasant surprises. By monitoring the feelings of those in power, he could mobilize support for desired initiatives in time to prevent serious setbacks. This knack for anticipating trouble was evident in his approach to securing the revenue-sharing agreement and gaining approval for construction projects.

DeBolt's attention to detail is legendary. Nothing is ever taken for granted. Subcontractors working on facilities projects learned this the hard way. DeBolt took it upon himself to regularly inspect every work site. When members of the leadership team were charged with planning major events and special ceremonies, they knew that DeBolt would always check to make certain that everything went off without a hitch. He never hired a member of his leadership team without making numerous phone calls to ensure that he was getting the right person for the job. While those who worked with DeBolt might enjoy a few laughs over his compulsiveness, they also understood that their boss was setting a high standard for their own administrative performance.

DeBolt's modeling did not stop at care for details. He exemplified the learning leader. Every year he always recommended several new books for leadership team members to read. He often observed that he himself had to learn about elementary education when he became superintendent, since his background was exclusively in secondary schools. And he just kept on learning. He learned about school construction and architecture, alternative ways to finance capital projects, and the best way to fertilize and maintain playing fields. DeBolt could forgive colleagues for not knowing something about schooling, but once they became aware of their lack of knowledge, they were expected to correct the situation. What was inexcusable was remaining unaware.

Reviewing DeBolt's first ten years as superintendent of Manassas Park City Schools, it is clear that two qualities of his personality served him—and the school system—particularly well. The qualities were patience and persistence, and both were necessary for effective leadership. Patience without persistence can be perceived as weakness. Persistence without patience risks undermining important relationships. Debolt's patience was manifested in his realization that the transformation of an entire school system cannot be achieved overnight. It takes time to build a coalition, elect supporters to the city council, and secure the resources necessary to build an effective organization. Though he rarely got everything he wanted immediately, DeBolt always kept pressing. He kept reminding people where the school system was headed and what it needed to get there. He let people know that he had no intention of bailing out when things got tough. He intended to stay the course until Manassas Park had a world-class school system.

DeBolt understands organizational change. He knows that boosting test scores for a year or two is one thing and sustaining success over a long period of time is quite another. He has no interest in "quick fixes" that might provide him with a launch pad to a bigger superintendency. Sustained success requires capital improvements, a talented corps of professionals, a dedicated leadership team, a supportive community, and ample resources. Most of all, however, it depends on stable and committed leadership at the top.

LESSON 8: TRANSFORMING A SCHOOL SYSTEM CAN TRANSFORM A COMMUNITY

Perhaps the most heartening lesson from Manassas Park concerns the impact of the school system's transformation on the community. When Tom DeBolt arrived in Manassas Park, the fledgling city struggled to attract middle-class families to its new subdivisions. Many of the school system's employees opted to live elsewhere. Manassas Park suffered in the shadow of its more affluent neighbor, the City of Manassas. Manassas Park epitomized the following characterization of school-community relations in urban settings:

[T]he stark reality of most urban schools is one of isolation and disconnection from the neighborhoods they serve. Most teachers and staff commute to their schools and have little understanding of, or connection with, the lives of their students outside of school, in their families and neighborhoods. (Warren, 2005, p. 136)

DeBolt's decision to purchase a home in the new Bloom's Crossing subdivision of Manassas Park symbolized his commitment to the community. He believed, and he convinced others to believe, that investing in the school system constituted an investment in Manassas Park's future. As each new school project was completed, as each set of improving test scores was published, as each athletic success was celebrated, the desirability of living in Manassas Park grew. Subdivisions filled and merchants created new businesses. By 2005, Manassas Park was considered an attractive place in which to live and work. Residents expressed pride in the quality of their schools and the education their children received. The transformation of Manassas Park City Schools was a key ingredient in the transformation of Manassas Park.

Notes

CHAPTER 1. INTRODUCTION

1. The methodology of organizational history is explained in greater detail in two previous books by the author: Daniel L. Duke, *The School That Refused to Die* (Albany: State University of New York Press, 1995) and Daniel L. Duke, *Education Empire: The Evolution of an Excellent Suburban School System*, (Albany: State University of New York Press, 2005).

CHAPTER 2. THE BIRTH OF A SCHOOL SYSTEM

1. An excellent source of information on the formation and early years of Manassas Park is David Glenn Melton's *A History of Manassas Park City Schools*, Doctoral Dissertation, Virginia Polytechnic Institute and State University, November 1998.

CHAPTER 6. A MATURING CULTURE OF HIGH ACHIEVEMENT

1. In April 2004, Manassas Park dedicated a new forty-one thousand square foot addition to the high school. The new wing expanded the school's capacity from 650 to 1,025 students. As with other projects, the school system relied on the architectural firm of VMDO. Input once again was solicited from teachers and students before completing the design.

References

CHAPTER 1

Bolman, L. G., & Deal, T. E. (1997). *Reframing organizations* (2nd ed.). San Francisco: Jossey-Bass.

2002 Census of Governments, Vol. 1, No. 1. (2002). Washington, D.C.: U.S. Department of Commerce, Bureau of the Census.

Stone, D. (1989). Causal stories and the formation of policy of policy agendas. *Political Science Quarterly 104(2)*, 281–300.

Tyack, D. & Cuban, L. (1995). *Tinkering toward utopia*. Cambridge: Harvard University Press.

CHAPTER 2

Annual Report 1976–1977: Superintendent of Public Instruction. (1977). Richmond: Virginia Department of Education.

Burns, P. (1988). Wren to school board: Boost test scores or resign. *Journal Messenger* (October 25), p. 1.

But they did it. (1976). *Journal Messenger* (September 14), p. 4A.

Call it quits. (1981). *Journal Messenger* (October 21), p. 4A.

Center for Applied Research and Development. (1989). Manassas Park City Public Schools Professional Development Project Phase One Report. Fairfax, VA: George Mason University.

Community sound off. (1975). *Journal Messenger* (April 30), p. 4A.

Curran, B. (1980). 53 Percent Park freshmen fail English. *Journal Messenger* (October 31), p. 1.

Curran, B. (1982). Park considers closing Connor. *Journal Messenger* (April 16), p. 1.

Curran, B. (1981). School called potential fire bomb. *Journal Messenger* (February 16), p. 1.

Curran, B. (1980). Two Manassas Park teachers failed more than 50 percent. *Journal Messenger* (June 24), p. 1.

Glier, R. (1983). Park council dissatisfied with school division. *Journal Messenger* (June 15), p. 1.

Leonard, D. (1976). Park picks Kentuckian to head school system. *Journal Messenger* (June 25), p. 1.

Manassas Park Town Council, Minutes (April 23, 1975).

Melton, D. G. (1998). *A history of Manassas Park City Schools.* Doctoral dissertation, Virginia Polytechnic Institute and State University.

Schein, E. H. (1985). *Organizational culture and leadership.* San Francisco: Jossey-Bass.

School Board Minutes, Manassas Park City Schools. September 18, 1980; March 19, 1981; July 7, 1983; February 7, 1985; December 15, 1988; December 21, 1989.

Turner, M. (1989). Teacher: MP schools run in "Mickey Mouse" fashion. *Journal Messenger* (March 13), p. 1.

Wolcott, V. (1994). Too close for comfort. *Journal Messenger* (November 1), p. 1.

Wren, David. (1985). City council orders school cuts. *Journal Messenger* (April 5), p. 1.

CHAPTER 3

Bhagwandin, S. (1998). A little off the top. *Journal Messenger* (March 5), pp. A1, A3.

Bhagwandin, S. (1999). High school students outdo themselves. *Journal Messenger* (July 30), p. A1.

Bhagwandin, S. (1998). Manassas Park cuts vocational programs. *Journal Messenger* (February 19), p. A2.

Bhagwandin, S. (1998). New standards challenge Manassas Park schools. *Journal Messenger* (January 26), pp. A1, A5.

Duke, D. L., & Reck, B. L. (2003). The evolution of educational accountability in the Old Dominion. In D. L. Duke, M. Grogan, P. D. Tucker, & W. Heinecke (Eds.), *Educational leadership in an age of accountability: The Virginia experience* (pp. 36–88). Albany: State University of New York Press.

Educational specifications: High school—650 students, Manassas Park City Schools, Manassas Park, Virginia. (1996). Bloomington, IN: KBD Planning Group, Inc.

Heisler, E. (1997). Manassas Park has mixed results. *Journal Messenger* (March 28), p. A-3.

Keilman, J. (1994). Superintendent Martin unveils Manassas Park school budget. *Journal Messenger* (February 17, 1994), p. A1.

Marino-Nachison, D. Many "ifs" surround Manassas Park School. *Journal Messenger* (February 1), p. A5.

Meixner, S. (1998). Manassas Park. *Journal Messenger* (January 7), pp. A-1, A-3.

Meixner, S. (1997). Manassas Park focus. *Journal Messenger* (October 30), p. A1.

Superintendent's annual report for Virginia, 1995–96. (1996). Richmond: Virginia Department of Education.

CHAPTER 4

Anderson, T. (1999). Manassas Park has highest rate of employment. *Journal Messenger* (January 14), p. A3.

Anderson, T. (1999). Manassas Park improves bond rating. *Journal Messenger* (March 19), p. A3.

Anderson, T. (1998). Manassas Park notebook. *Journal Messenger* (September 10), p. A1.

Bhagwandin, S. (1999). Manassas Park officials are still hoping for new school. *Journal Messenger* (January 14), p. A3.

Bhagwandin, S. (1998). Manassas Park scouts site for schools. *Journal Messenger* (September 15), pp. A1, A3.

Bhagwandin, S. (1999). New Manassas Park school not high on budget priorities. *Journal Messenger* (January 18), pp. A1, A4.

Cannon, L. (2002). School's student-friendly design wins praise. *Journal Messenger* (January 9), p. A3.

Daughtery, R. (1998). Manassas Park debates school site. *Journal Messenger* (November 13), p. A3.

Daugherty, R. (1998). School site in Manassas Park sparks debate. *Journal Messenger* (November 11), p. A1.

Doherty, P. (2000). New elementary on time, within budget. *Journal Messenger* (January 20), p. A3.

Newman, C. (2000). Manassas Park posts a $2 million surplus. *Journal Messenger* (December 1), p. A3.

News brief. (1999). *Journal Messenger* (March 5), p. A3.

Report of the peer review team for Cougar Elementary School. (2003). Southern Association of Colleges and Schools, October 13–14.

Rettig, M. D. (2006). Letter of support (February 4), National School Change Awards, Fordham University.

School renewal summary report: Cougar Elementary School, 1997–2003. (2003). Manassas Park: Manassas Park City Schools.

Schwab, T. (2000). Cougar Elementary. *Journal Messenger* (November 16), pp. A1, A3.

CHAPTER 5

Bhagwandin, S. (1998). Manassas Park schools create five-year budget. *Journal Messenger* (October 1), p. A3.

Division goals. (1996). Manassas Park City Schools.

Parrish, T. N. (2004). M. Park, school board reach revenue agreement. *Journal Messenger* (January 23), pp. A1–A2.

Summary of local financial contributions to select Northern Virginia school districts. (2003). Arlington, VA: Public Financial Management.

Technology plan: 2003–2009. (n.d.). Manassas Park City Schools.

2005–2006 salary schedules for teachers: Vol. I: Benchmarks and rankings. (2005). Richmond: Virginia Education Association.

Vision, mission, goals, and objectives, Six-year plan, 2001–2007. (2000). Manassas Park City Schools.

CHAPTER 6

Deal, T. E., & Kennedy, A. A. (1982). *Corporate cultures*. Reading, MA: Addison-Wesley.

Manassas Park city schools: The transformation of a school division, 1994–2006. (2006). A PowerPoint presentation to the city council.

Parrish, T. N. (2004). Manassas Park middle school to get expansion, renovation. *Journal Messenger* (August 17), p. A5.

Parrish, T. N. (2004). Schools reinforce character. *Journal Messenger* (October 26), pp. A1–A2.

Schein, E. H. (1985). *Organizational culture and leadership*. San Francisco: Jossey-Bass.

School board minutes, Manassas Park City Schools, February 22, 2005.

Vision, mission, goals, and objectives. Six-year plan, 2001–2007. (2000). Manassas Park: Manassas Park City Schools.

CHAPTER 7

Cohn, D'V., & Gardner, A. (2006). 3 outer VA suburbs near top of U.S. in growth. *Washington Post* (March 16), p. A1.

Gilbert, D. (2006). Hispanics Discuss Hardships. *Journal Messenger* (January 26), pp. A1–A2.

Gladwell, M. (2002). *The tipping point*. Boston: Little, Brown.

McCrummen, S. (2005). Manassas changes definition of family. *Washington Post* (December 28), pp. A1, A5.

McCrummen, S. (2006). Manassas suspends residency restriction. *Washington Post* (January 5), pp. B1, B5.

School board minutes, Manassas Park City Schools, June 6, 2005.

Seal, R. (2005). Manassas Park council cuts tax rate. *Journal Messenger* (October 12), p. A1.

Shapira, I. (2006). Reeling from test results, N.Va. educators regroup. *Washington Post* (September 2), p. B5.

Stewart, A. M. (2006). Park candidates get schooled. *Journal Messenger* (April 18), pp. A1, A2.

Stewart, N. (2005). Hurricane victims'Va. refuge proves only temporary. *Washington Post* (December 10), pp. B1, B5.

CHAPTER 8

Adler, P. S., & Borys, B. (1996). Two types of bureaucracy: Enabling and coercive. *Administrative Science Quarterly, 41(1)*, 61–89.

Bista, M., & Glasman, N. S. (1998). Principals' approaches to leadership, their antecedents, and student outcomes. *Journal of School Leadership, 8(3)* (March), 109–136.

Bolman, L. G. & Deal, T. E. (1997). *Reframing organizations* (2nd ed.). San Francisco: Jossey-Bass.

Bridges, W. (2004). *Transitions* (2nd ed.). Cambridge, MA: DaCapo Press.

Duke, D. L. (2004). *The challenges of educational change*. Boston: Allyn & Bacon.

Hall, G. E., & Hord, S. M. (2001). *Implementing change*. Boston: Allyn & Bacon.

Hoy, W. K., & Sweetland, S. R. (2001). Designing better schools: The meaning and measure of enabling school structures. *Educational Administration Quarterly, 37(3)* (August), 296–321.

CHAPTER 9

Bodilly, S. (1996). Lessons learned. In S. Stringfield, S. Ross, & L. Smith (Eds.), *Bold plans for school restructuring* (pp. 289–324). Mahwah, NJ: Erlbaum.

Brouillette, L. (1996). *A geology of school reform*. Albany: State University of New York Press.

Childress, S., Elmore, R., & Grossman, A. (2006). How to manage urban school districts. *Harvard Business Review, 84(11)* (November), 55–68.

Darling-Hammond, L., Hightower, A., Husbands, J. L., LaFors, J. R., Young, V. M., & Christopher, C. (2003). Building instructional quality: "Inside-out" and "outside-in" perspectives on San Diego's school reform: A research report. Seattle: Center for the Study of Teaching and Policy, University of Washington.

Duke, D. L. (2004). *The challenges of educational change*. Boston: Pearson.

Duke, D. L. (1998). Does it matter where our children learn? Paper commissioned by the National Research Council of the National Academy of Sciences and the National Academy of Engineering. Washington, DC: National Research Council.

Hightower, A. (2002). San Diego's big boom: Systemic instructional change in the central office and schools. In A. Hightower, M. Knapp, J. A. Marsh, and M. W. McLaughlin (Eds.), *School districts and instructional renewal* (pp. 76–93). New York: Teachers College Press.

Hill, P. T.; Campbell, C., & Harvey, J. (2000). *It takes a city.* Washington, DC: Brookings.

Jones, D. (2006). Schools take a lesson from big business. *USA Today* (March 9), pp. B-1, B-2.

Kohn, A. (1999). *The schools our children deserve.* Boston: Houghton Mifflin.

Lindblom, C. E. (1980). *The policy-making process* (2nd ed.). Englewood Cliffs, NJ: Prentice-Hall.

Marsh, J. A. (2002). How districts relate to states, schools, and communities: A review of emerging literature. In A. Hightower, M. Knapp, J. A. Marsh, & M. W. McLaughlin (Eds.), *School districts and instructional renewal* (pp. 25–40). New York: Teachers College Press.

McLaughlin, M. W. (1990). The Rand change agent study revisited: Macro perspectives and micro realities. *Educational Researcher, 19(9)* (December), 11–15.

McLaughlin, M. W., & Talbert, J. E. (2002). Reforming districts. In A. Hightower, M. Knapp, J. A. Marsh, & M. W. McLaughlin (Eds.), *School districts and instructional renewal* (pp. 173–192). New York: Teachers College Press.

Muncey, D. E., & McQuillan, P. J. (1996). *Reform and resistance in schools and classrooms.* New Haven: Yale.

Ohanian, S. (1999). *One size fits few.* Portsmouth, NH: Heinemann.

Romanelli, E., & Tushman, M. L. (1994). Organizational transformation as punctuated equilibrium: An empirical test. *The Academy of Management Journal 37(5)* (October), 1141–1166.

Warren, M. R. (2005). Communities and schools: A new view of urban education reform. *Harvard Educational Review 75(2)* (Summer), 133–173.

Index

170 Index